John R. Sweney

Songs of Love and Praise No. 5

For use in Meetings for Christian Worship or Work

John R. Sweney

Songs of Love and Praise No. 5
For use in Meetings for Christian Worship or Work

ISBN/EAN: 9783337182052

Printed in Europe, USA, Canada, Australia, Japan

Cover: Foto ©Thomas Meinert / pixelio.de

More available books at **www.hansebooks.com**

SONGS OF
LOVE AND PRAISE
No. 5

FOR USE IN

Meetings for Christian Worship

or Work

EDITORS:

JOHN R. SWENEY   J. HOWARD ENTWISLE

AND THE LATE

FRANK M. DAVIS

JOHN J. HOOD

PHILADELPHIA: 1024 Arch Street   CHICAGO: 940 W. Madison Street

Copyright, 1898, by John J. Hood

EXALTED theme! Sublimest of emotions,
　　The love of God, enthroned above the sky;
Broader than all the earth's united oceans,
　　Older than time, vast as eternity;
Beyond the deepest depths, and highest heights,
The matchless central source of heaven's supreme delights.

O for a song and voice of love's inspiring,
　　With which to fill the earth and heaven above;
For strength to speed on lofty wings, untiring,
　　Swifter than light, proclaiming holy love
In songs of tenderness divinely sweet,
Till universes bow at the Redeemer's feet.

　　　　　　　　　　　　E. H. S.

COPYRIGHT NOTICE

To print any copyright hymn or tune of this collection for any purpose, unless written permission shall have been obtained from the owner thereof, is an infringement of the copyright law.　　　　　　　　　　　　THE PUBLISHER.

No. 5.
SONGS OF LOVE AND PRAISE.

The Wonderful Saviour.

F. M. D.
Frank M. Davis.

1. Christ has shed his blood for me, O what a wonderful Sav-iour!
2. I have lost my load of sin, O what a wonderful Sav-iour!
3. Now my heart doth sing for joy, O what a wonderful Sav-iour!

Died my soul from sin to free, O what a wonderful Sav-iour!
Now I have sweet peace within, O what a wonderful Sav-iour!
Christ shall all my song employ, O what a wonderful Sav-iour!

Greater love was nev-er known, Greater mer-cy nev-er shown;
He who calm-ly walk'd the wave Has the mighty pow'r to save,
He my guide, my strength and stay, All my tears has wiped a-way;

Free-ly does his blood a-tone, O what a wonderful Sav-iour!
Shows a light beyond the grave, O what a wonderful Sav-iour!
I will serve him ev-'ry day, O what a wonderful Sav-iour!

Copyright, 1896, by Frank M. Davis. John J. Hood, owner.

(3)

Moment by Moment.

D. W. WHITTLE.   2 Cor. iv: 17.   Miss M. WHITTLE.

1. Dy-ing with Je-sus, by death reckon'd mine; Liv-ing with Je-sus, a new life di-vine; Looking to Je-sus till glo-ry doth shine, Moment by moment, O Lord, I am thine.

2. Nev-er a bat-tle with wrong for the right, Never a contest that he doth not fight; Lifting a-bove us his banner so white, Moment by moment I'm kept in his sight.

3. Nev-er a tri-al that he is not there, Nev-er a burden that he doth not bear; Nev-er a sorrow that he doth not share, Moment by moment I'm under his care.

CHORUS.

Moment by moment I'm kept in his love; Moment by moment I've life from a-bove; Looking to Je-sus till glo-ry doth shine; Moment by moment, O Lord, I am thine.

Copyright, 1893, by The Biglow & Main Co. Used by per.

4 Never a heartache, and never a groan,
Never a teardrop, and never a moan;
Never a danger but there on the throne,
Moment by moment he thinks of his own.

5 Never a weakness that he doth not feel,
Never a sickness that he cannot heal;
Moment by moment, in woe or in weal,
Jesus, my Saviour, abides with me still.

Only Once You Pass this Way.

Rev. Johnson Oatman, Jr.
Jno. R. Sweney.

1. Do your best while life's pilgrim way you tread, Scatt'ring sunshine while you [may;
2. Ev'ry day poor and needy you will find, Fill'd with sorrow and dismay;
3. Tell the world that the Saviour died for all, Bid them ever watch and pray;
4. Be a brave, earnest soldier in the strife, Then when comes the close of day,

Bear in mind, while the precious seed you spread, On-ly once you pass this way.
Do your best some poor, broken hearts to bind, On-ly once you pass this way.
Lift your voice, shout aloud the gospel call, On-ly once you pass this way.
May the world be the better for your life, On-ly once you pass this way.

CHORUS.

Only once you pass this way, Only once you pass this way;
On-ly once you pass this way, only once you pass this way;

Be a blessing while you may, Only once you pass this way.
Be a blessing, be a blessing while you may,

Copyright, 1890, by Jno. R. Sweney.

Fully Justified.

F. M. D.
Frank M. Davis.

1. Thro' our faith in Christ the Lord we are justi-fied, Ful-ly jus-ti-fied,
2. He has opened wide the door and we've entered in, Ful-ly jus-ti-fied,
3. We who know our sins forgiv'n in the Lord rejoice, Ful-ly jus-ti-fied,

ful-ly jus-ti-fied; Thro' the all - a - toning blood of the Cru-ci-fied,
ful-ly jus-ti-fied; He a-lone has set us free from the bonds of sin,
ful-ly jus-ti-fied; We will swell abroad his praise with a mighty voice,

CHORUS.

Ful-ly justified, ful-ly justified. Ful - ly jus - ti - fied,
Ful-ly jus-ti-fied, ful-ly jus-ti-fied,

Tell it out, sing it out, Spread it far and wide; Thro' the all - a - toning

blood of the Cru-ci-fied, Ful-ly jus-ti-fied, ful-ly jus-ti-fied.

Copyright, 1896, by Frank M. Davis. John J. Hood, owner.

Will You be One?—CONCLUDED.

Ev- er rejoic- ing at Jesus' right hand, Will you be one? . . .
Will you be one by and by?

Wait On the Lord.

FANNY J. CROSBY. JNO. R. SWENEY.

1. Wait on the Lord, wait patient- ly, And thou shalt in him be blest;
2. Wait on the Lord, wait cheerfully, And he will thy youth re - new;
3. Wait on the Lord, wait loving- ly, Confide in his care thy all;
4. Wait on the Lord, wait joyful- ly, For then shall thy heart be strong;

Fine.

Aft- er the storm, a ho - ly calm, And aft- er thy la - bor, rest.
Wait on the Lord o - bedient - ly, Whatev- er he bids thee do.
Those that a- bide in perfect peace No danger can e'er be - fall.
Lo! by his hand he leadeth thee, And thou shalt be fill'd with song.

D.S.—O- ver thy soul a watch he keeps, Wherever thy path may be.

CHORUS. D.S.

Wait on the Lord, for whom hast thou On earth or in heaven but he? . . .
but he?

Copyright, 1887, by Jno. R. Sweney.

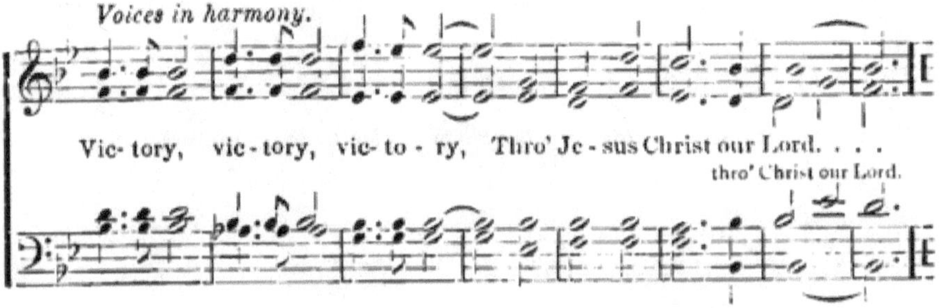

The Joyful Song.—CONCLUDED.

Voices in harmony.

Vic-tory, vic-tory, vic-to-ry, Thro' Je-sus Christ our Lord....
thro' Christ our Lord.

The Blood is On the Lintel.

"And when I see the blood, I will pass over you."—Ex. xii: 13.

Rev. E. A. Hoffman.   Jno. R. Bryant.

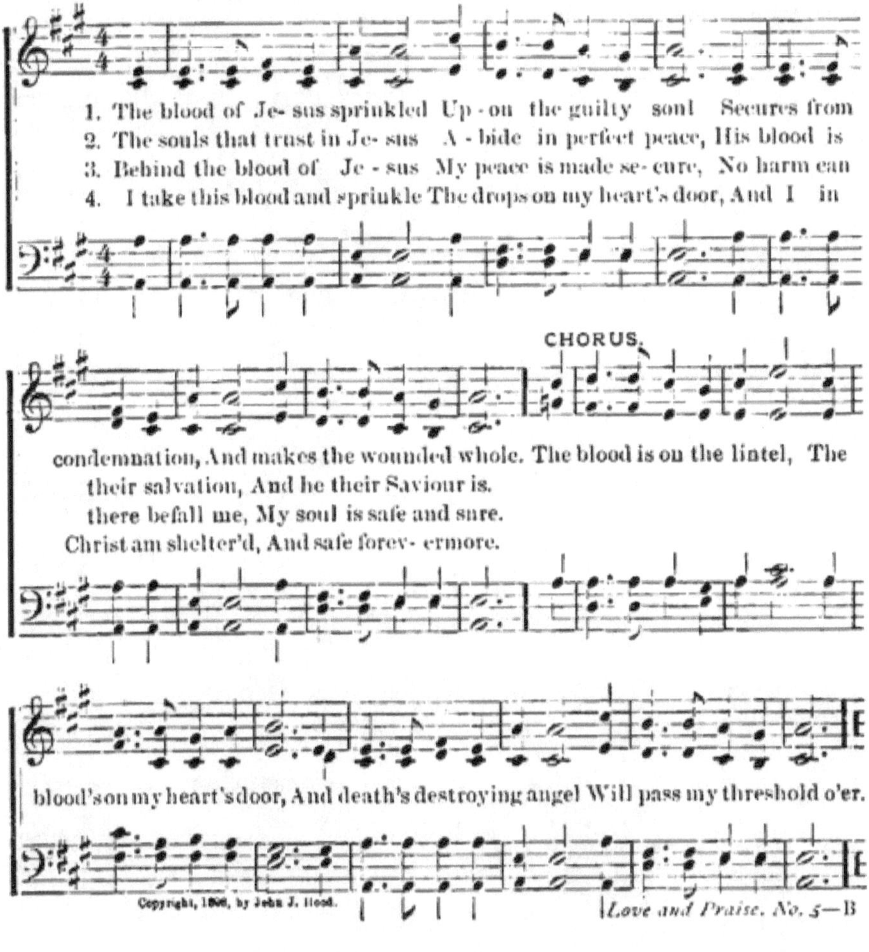

1. The blood of Je-sus sprinkled Up-on the guilty soul Secures from
2. The souls that trust in Je-sus A-bide in perfect peace, His blood is
3. Behind the blood of Je-sus My peace is made se-cure, No harm can
4. I take this blood and sprinkle The drops on my heart's door, And I in

CHORUS.

condemnation, And makes the wounded whole. The blood is on the lintel, The
their salvation, And he their Saviour is.
there befall me, My soul is safe and sure.
Christ am shelter'd, And safe forev-ermore.

blood's on my heart's door, And death's destroying angel Will pass my threshold o'er.

Copyright, 1896, by John J. Hood.   *Love and Praise. No. 5*—B

Crossing One by One.—CONCLUDED.

ev-er to a-bide,—We shall cross the mystic riv-er, one by one.

The Life on Wings.

Mrs. Frank A. Breck.   Jno. R. Sweney.

1. My soul, stay not in shadows, Where the mist of sorrow clings; There is
2. On wings of faith mount upward, Far beyond all earthly things; There is
3. There's triumph in all trial, 'Tis the peace that Jesus brings; O'er the

joy for the heart bidding shadows depart, There is joy for the life on wings.
peace that will last till thy journey is past, There is joy for the life on wings.
faith-mounted soul sorrow hath no control, There is joy for the life on wings.

CHORUS.

Mount up, my soul, with gladness, Where the sunshine cheers and warms;

The life on wings is the life that sings, Then soar above the storms.

Copyright, 1896, by Jno. R. Sweney.

Sunshine of the Saviour's, etc.—CONCLUDED.   23

glorious, heavenly sunshine, Sunshine in the sweetness of the Saviour's smile.

I Shall Be Like Him.

W. A. S.   Rev. W. A. Spencer, D.D.

1. When I shall reach the more excellent glory, And all my trials are passed,
2. We shall not wait till the glorious dawning Breaks on the vision so fair,
3. More and more like him, repeat the blest story, Over and o-ver a-gain,

I shall behold him, O wonderful story!   I shall be like him at last.
Now we may welcome the heavenly morning, Now we his image may bear.
Changed by his spirit from glory to glory, I shall be sat-isfied then.

CHORUS.

I shall be like him,   I shall be like him, And in his beauty shall shine;

I shall be like him, wondrously like him, Jesus, my Saviour di-vine.

Copyright, 1897, by W. A. Spencer. Used by permission.

Nearer every Day.—CONCLUDED.

For I see the lights of home, And I'm getting nearer, nearer ev'ry day.

Dwelling in Love.

Rev. Wm. Underwood.   Jno. R. Sweney.

1. In love di-vine I dwell, The Spirit gives the pow'r; My God is
2. I therefore dwell in God, He makes my heart his home; A-live on
3. My soul, once starving, feeds On hidden manna giv'n; My God sup-
4. Tho' storms my soul assail, Thro' hope, steadfast and sure, My anchor,

D.S.—My God is

CHORUS.

love, I know it well, He saves me hour by hour. He saves me
earth, or 'neath the sod I'm his, and his a-lone.
plies my pres-ent needs And prom-i-ses me heav'n.
cast with-in the vale,— I ride the waves se-cure.

love, I know it well, He saves me hour by hour.

now, . . . I feel his mighty pow'r, He saves, he saves . . this very hour;

5 Nor life, nor death alarms
  The saints whom God indues;
  Die they? In everlasting arms
  Eternal life ensues.

6 Free grace to fallen man
  I'll sing in heav'n above;
  Excell me, angels, if you can!
  Saved by redeeming love.

34. Who will Answer for Me?

The late Rev. Daniel Curry once dreamed that he had died and gone to Judgment. As he stood trembling before the bar, the Judge asked this question, "Who will answer for Daniel Curry?" Then he heard the sweet voice of Jesus reply, "I will answer for him."

Rev. Johnson Oatman, Jr. J. Howard Entwisle.

1. Who will answer for me, when, life's battles all past, I shall stand at the bar of the Judgment at last, When before me the Judge of all nations I see, In that terrible hour, who will answer for me?

2. Oh, how dark all my past, as from there I look back, Many sins and mistakes will I count on my track, Scarce a single good deed on my record I see, And I cry in despair, "who will answer for me?"

3. Justice there will I see with the scales in her hand, And I know I shall quake as upon them I stand; "Weigh'd and found wanting" there, as no doubt I shall be In my weakness and fear;—who will answer for me?

4. Saviour, help me to walk close to thee day by day, When I hear thy commands may I trust and obey; While I live may I ever to thee faithful be, Then at last hear thee say, "I will answer for thee!"

D.S.—answer for this guilty soul?" Then my Saviour will turn with compassion t'ward me, And his sweet voice will say, "I will answer for thee!"

CHORUS.

When the Judge shall at last call my name from the roll, And shall ask, "who will answer for this guilty soul?" Then my Saviour will turn with compassion t'ward me, And his sweet voice will say, "I will answer for thee!"

Copyright, 1898, by John J. Hood.

The Sweet, Glad Time.

"Let us labor therefore to enter into that rest."—Heb. iv: 11.

F. M. D.
Frank M. Davis.

1. We shall reach . . . the land of light, In the sweet, glad time by and by;
2. We shall join . . . the angel throng, In the sweet, glad time by and by;
3. We shall lay . . . our crosses down, In the sweet, glad time by and by;

1. We shall reach the land of light,

There will fall . . . no shades of night, In the sweet, glad time by and by.
We shall sing . . . the new, new song, In the sweet, glad time by and by.
We shall wear . . . the victor's crown, In the sweet, glad time by and by.

There will fall no shades of night,

CHORUS.

By and by, by and by, In the sweet, glad time by and by;

By and by, by and by, by and by;

We shall reach . . . the land of light, In the sweet, glad time by and by.

We shall reach the land of light,

From "Songs of Praise." By per. of John J. Hood.

Just One Touch.

BIRDIE BELL.
J. HOWARD ENTWISLE.

SOLO. *Slow, with expression.*

1. Just one touch as he moves along, Push'd and press'd by the jostling throng,
2. Just one touch and he makes me whole, Speaks sweet peace to my sin-sick soul,
3. Just one touch! and the work is done, I am saved by the blessed Son,
4. Just one touch! and he turns to me, O the love in his eyes I see!
5. Just one touch! by his mighty pow'r, He can heal thee this ver-y hour,

Just one touch and the weak was strong, Cured by the Healer di-vine.
At his feet all my burdens roll,—Cured by the Healer di-vine.
I will sing while the a-ges run, Cured by the Healer di-vine.
I am his for he hears my plea, Cured by the Healer di-vine.
Thou canst hear tho' the tempests low'r, Cured by the Healer di-vine.

CHORUS.

Just one touch as he pass-es by, He will list to the faintest cry,

Come and be saved while the Lord is nigh, Christ is the Healer di-vine.

Copyright, 1897, by J. Howard Entwisle.

44. The Song that Never shall Die.

Ida Scott Taylor.   J. Howard Entwisle.

1. A glorious song is ringing in my heart, Its joyous notes new life and hope impart, It fills me with its sweetness, Gladness and completeness, 'Tis the love of God that tunes my tongue,—Wonderful love! "All glory to God on high!"
2. I came because the Lord has cleans'd my sin, And by his blood has wash'd me white with-in, I sing the blessed story, Sing of Christ my glory, 'Tis the love of God that makes me sing,—Wonderful love!
3. O blessed song that nevermore shall die, The world shall know its meaning by and by, I'll keep its music ringing, With triumphant singing, 'Tis the love of God that thrills my soul,—Wonderful love!

CHORUS.

O song of hope and gladness That thrills the earth and sky, I'll sing it o'er for-ev-ermore, The song that never shall die.

Copyright, 1897, 1898, by John J. Hood.

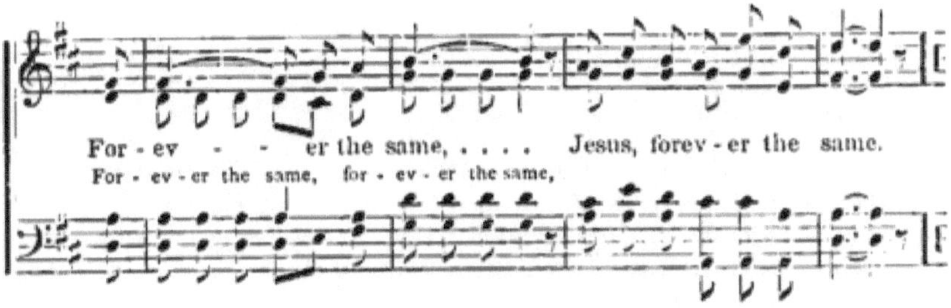

Jesus, Forever the Same.—CONCLUDED.

47

For-ev-er the same, ... Jesus, forev-er the same.
For-ev-er the same, for-ev-er the same,

He Fills it All.

Rev. Johnson Oatman, Jr.   J. Howard Entwisle.

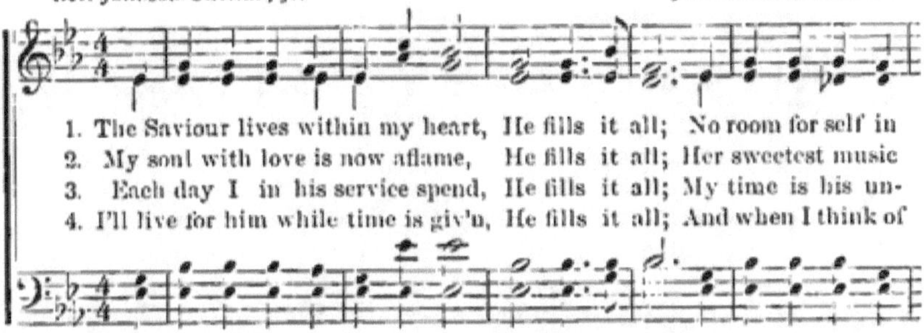

1. The Saviour lives within my heart, He fills it all; No room for self in
2. My soul with love is now aflame, He fills it all; Her sweetest music
3. Each day I in his service spend, He fills it all; My time is his un-
4. I'll live for him while time is giv'n, He fills it all; And when I think of

CHORUS.

an-y part, He fills it all.   Jesus fills it all,   Yes, Je-sus
is his name, He fills it all.
til the end, He fills it all.
yonder heav'n, He fills it all.

he fills it all,

fills it all; My life is swallow'd up in him,—He fills it all.
he fills it all;

Copyright, 1893, by John J. Hood.

Sweeter as the Days go By.

E. E. Hewitt.
Jno. R. Sweney.

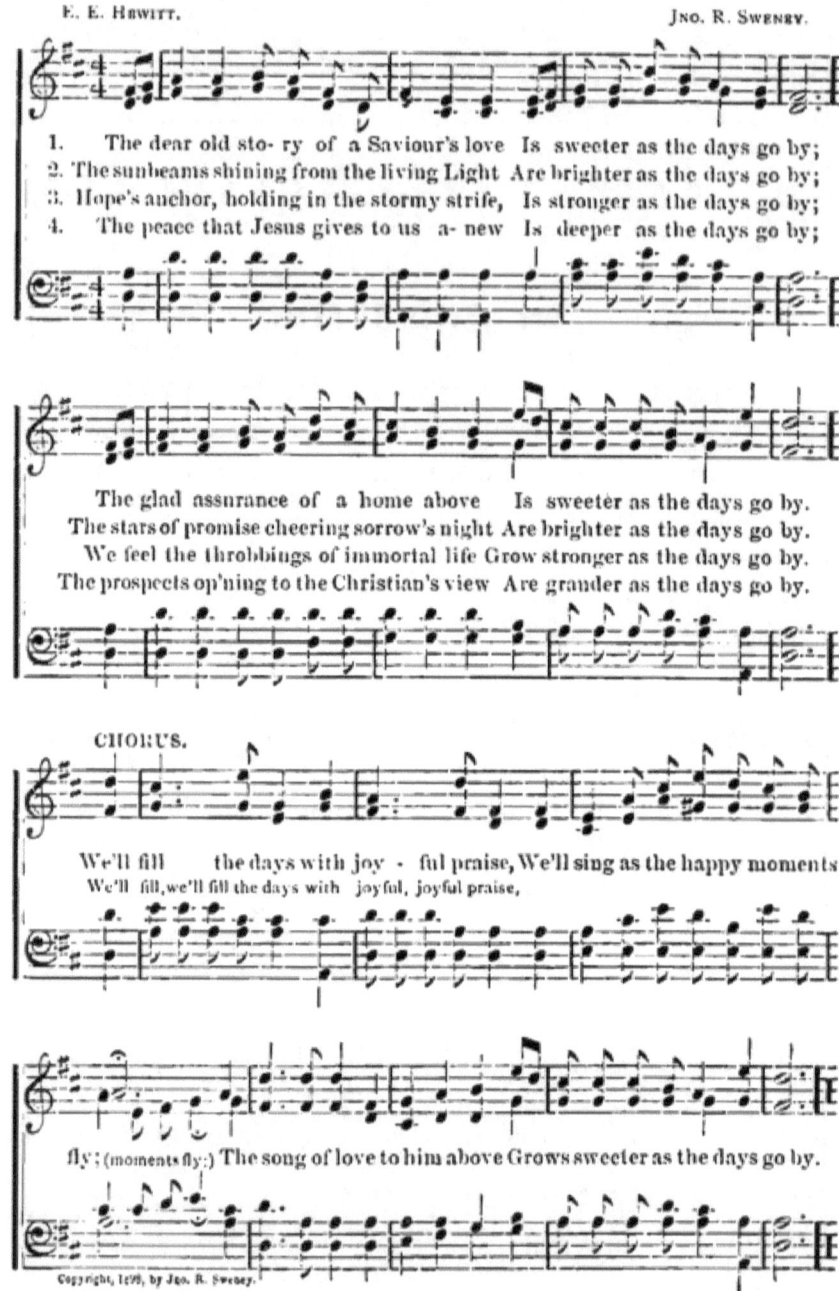

1. The dear old sto-ry of a Saviour's love Is sweeter as the days go by;
2. The sunbeams shining from the living Light Are brighter as the days go by;
3. Hope's anchor, holding in the stormy strife, Is stronger as the days go by;
4. The peace that Jesus gives to us a-new Is deeper as the days go by;

The glad assurance of a home above Is sweeter as the days go by.
The stars of promise cheering sorrow's night Are brighter as the days go by.
We feel the throbbings of immortal life Grow stronger as the days go by.
The prospects op'ning to the Christian's view Are grander as the days go by.

CHORUS.

We'll fill the days with joy - ful praise, We'll sing as the happy moments
We'll fill, we'll fill the days with joyful, joyful praise,

fly; (moments fly:) The song of love to him above Grows sweeter as the days go by.

Copyright, 1899, by Jno. R. Sweney.

On to Victory.—CONCLUDED.

Onward in the conflict, hop-ing, trusting, On to vic-to-ry!

Be of Good Cheer.

CHARLOTTE ABBEY. "Be of good cheer; It is I; be not afraid."—Mark vi: 6o. FRANK M. DAVIS.

1. "Be of good cheer," saith the Saviour, "Tho' all thy brightest hopes fade;
2. "Be of good cheer, tho' the tempter And world are 'gainst thee array'd;
3. "Be of good cheer thro' thy tri-als; On me let burdens be laid;

I will be near to sus-tain thee; It is I, O be not a-fraid."
I will give grace that will conquer; It is I, O be not a-fraid."
Tho' they be heavy, I'll bear them; It is I, O be not a-fraid."

CHORUS.

It is I, ... it is I, ... It is I, O be not a-fraid!
It is I, it is I,

"Be of good cheer," saith the Saviour; "It is I, O be not a-fraid!"

From "Notes of Praise." By per. of John J. Hood.

When the Roll is Called, etc.—CONCLUDED. 53

roll .. is called up yonder, When the roll is called up yonder, I'll be there.

Lord, I'm Coming Home.

W. J. K. *With great feeling.* WM. J. KIRKPATRICK.

1. I've wandered far a-way from God, Now I'm coming home;
2. I've wast-ed ma-ny pre-cious years, Now I'm coming home;
3. I'm tired of sin and stray-ing, Lord, Now I'm coming home;
4. My soul is sick, my heart is sore, Now I'm coming home;

The paths of sin too long I've trod, Lord, I'm coming home.
I now re-pent with bit-ter tears, Lord, I'm coming home.
I'll trust thy love, be-lieve thy word, Lord, I'm coming home.
My strength renew, my hope re-store, Lord, I'm coming home.

D.S.—O-pen wide thine arms of love, Lord, I'm coming home.

CHORUS.

Coming home, coming home, Nev-er more to roam;

Copyright, 1892, by Wm. J. Kirkpatrick.

5 My only hope, my only plea,
  Now I'm coming home,
That Jesus died, and died for me,
  Lord, I'm coming home.

6 I need his cleansing blood I know,
  Now I'm coming home;
Oh, wash me whiter than the snow,
  Lord, I'm coming home.

Journey in the King's, etc.—CONCLUDED. 59

Come, in shining robes be clad, And go singing in the King's highway.

Unto His Marvellous Light.

F. E. Hewitt. Jno. R. Sweney.

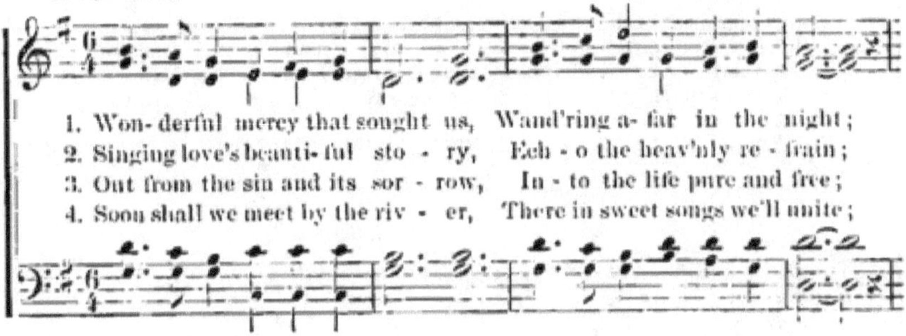

1. Won-derful mercy that sought us, Wand'ring a-far in the night;
2. Singing love's beauti-ful sto-ry, Ech-o the heav'nly re-frain;
3. Out from the sin and its sor-row, In-to the life pure and free;
4. Soon shall we meet by the riv-er, There in sweet songs we'll unite;

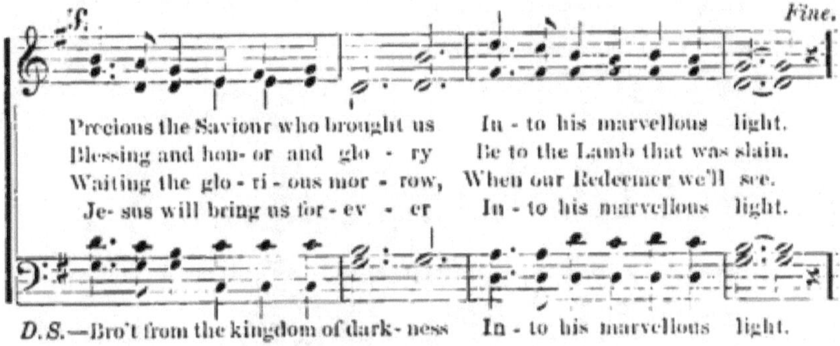

Precious the Saviour who brought us In-to his marvellous light.
Blessing and hon-or and glo-ry Be to the Lamb that was slain.
Waiting the glo-ri-ous mor-row, When our Redeemer we'll see.
Je-sus will bring us for-ev-er In-to his marvellous light.

D. S.—Bro't from the kingdom of dark-ness In-to his marvellous light.

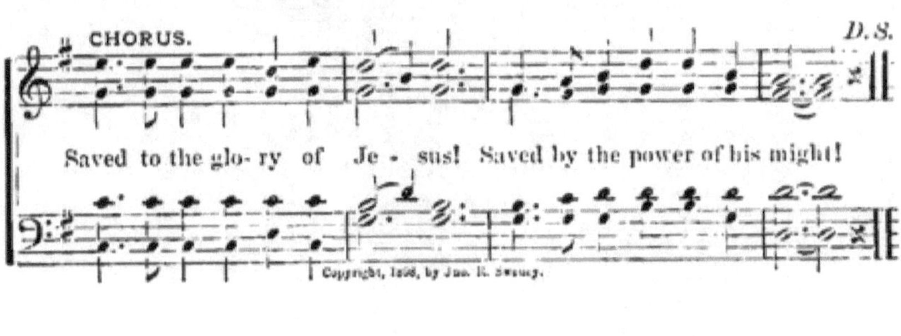

CHORUS. D. S.

Saved to the glo-ry of Je-sus! Saved by the power of his might!

Copyright, 1896, by Jno. R. Sweney.

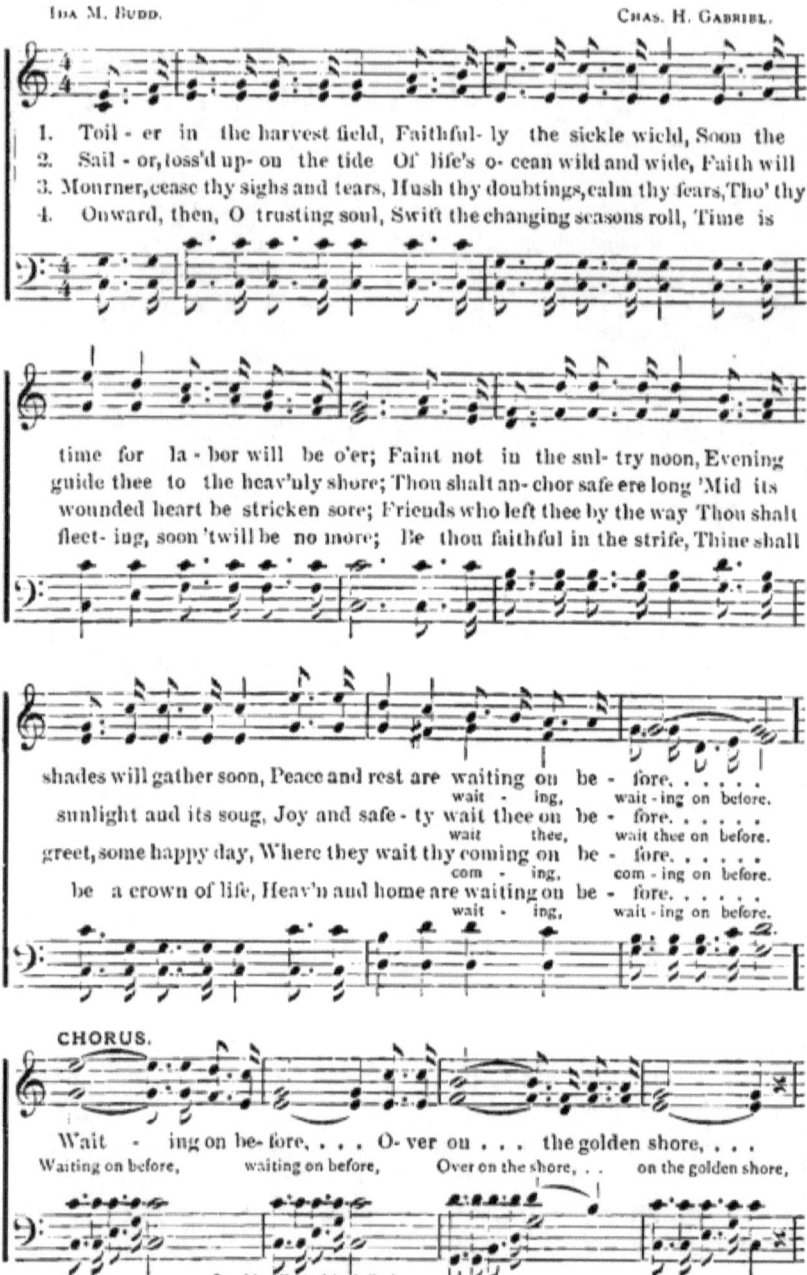

Waiting on Before.—CONCLUDED.

Shines ... the perfect, heav'nly day, Where the blest shall dwell forevermore.
Shines the perfect day, perfect, heav'nly day,

There's Gain for All Our Losses.

"And God shall wipe away all tears."—Rev. xxi: 4.

Mrs. ANNIE E. THOMSON. FRANK M. DAVIS.

Gently.

1. There's gain for all our loss-es, By and by, by and by; There's ease from
2. There's bliss for all our sigh-ing, By and by, by and by; No want, or
3. Then smiles for all our weeping, By and by, by and by; And lov'd ones
4. There's love for all our long-ing By and by, by and by; Where an-gel

all our crosses, By and by, by and by; There's freedom from each care, And
pain or sighing, By and by, by and by; No rugged paths we'll go, No
lonely sleeping, By and by, by and by, Shall one day with us rise To
hosts are thronging, By and by, by and by; With golden harps we'll sing Glad

burdens that we bear, When heav'n's blest joys we'll share, By and by, by and by.
cherish'd hope laid low, No wounded spir-it know, By and by, by and by.
glories of the skies, Where pleasure never dies, By and by, by and by.
praise to Christ our King, Till heav'nly courts shall ring, By and by, by and by.

Love and Praise, No. 5—E From "New Pearls of Song." By per. of John J. Hood.

Who Can Tell?—CONCLUDED.

sleeping where the soft wind blows, But his soul is in heaven, safe with God.
sleeping where the soft wind blows, But her soul is in heaven, safe with God.
sleeping where the soft wind blows, But his soul is in heaven, safe with God.
sleeping where the soft wind blows, But her soul is in heaven, safe with God.
sleeping where the soft wind blows, But their souls are in heaven, safe with God.

Give Me the Mind of Jesus.

IDA SCOTT TAYLOR. JNO. R. SWENEY.

1. Give me the mind of Je - sus, Purer than lilies white, Give me his gentle
2. Give me his tender pit - y, Tho' but a word I speak, Let me, O heav'nly
3. Give me the grace of Je - sus, Help me the cross to bear, Casting on him my

CHORUS.

spir - it, Help me to live aright.
Father, Comfort the sad and weak. Oh, to be more like Je - sus, This is the
burden, Leaving with him my care.

pray'r I pray; Loving and serving him always, Trusting him day by day.

Copyright, 1896, by Jno. R. Sweney.

The Streets of Gold.

Jesse P. Tompkins.   J. Howard Entwisle.

SOLO OR DUET.

1. When the skies are low'ring, Saviour dear, And thorns bestrew my way. I'd
2. When the sun is shining, Saviour dear, And all around is fair, When
3. When the night is falling, Saviour dear, May I in thee a-bide, And

QUARTET.

hold thy hand in grief and pain, Thou art my hope and stay; Thro' mists that inter-
roses flush'd with beauty bright, Shed perfume on the air, Oh, may I praise thy
hear thy gentle voice, in love, Say, "I am by thy side;" "The night will not be

vene, Lord, Oh, lead me to thy fold, Where weary feet may rest, Lord, And
name, Lord, For all thy love un-told, And pray that I may see thee, And
long, child, The dawn will soon unfold, And I will lead thee home, child, To

to thy fold,

CHORUS.

tread the streets of gold. When the morn is breaking, And joys supreme un-
tread the streets of gold.
tread the streets of gold."

fold; . . Oh, may I clasp thy sacred hands, And tread the streets of gold.
unfold;   the streets of gold.

Copyright, 1888, by John J. Hood.

Caring for Me.

71

E. E. Hewitt.   J. Howard Entwisle.

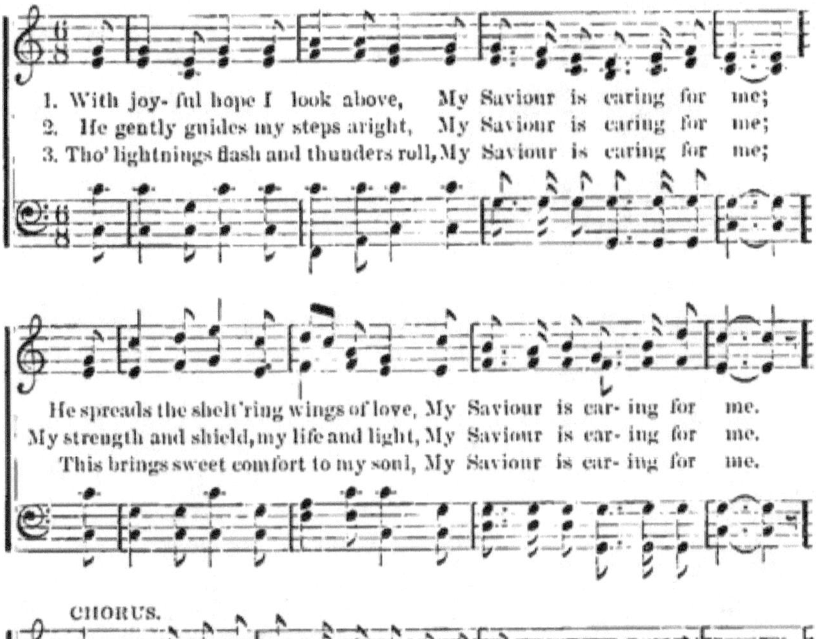

1. With joyful hope I look above, My Saviour is caring for me;
2. He gently guides my steps aright, My Saviour is caring for me;
3. Tho' lightnings flash and thunders roll, My Saviour is caring for me;

He spreads the shelt'ring wings of love, My Saviour is caring for me.
My strength and shield, my life and light, My Saviour is caring for me.
This brings sweet comfort to my soul, My Saviour is caring for me.

CHORUS.

Caring, so tenderly caring, My Saviour is caring for me;
Caring for me, for me;

Caring, so faithfully caring, My Saviour is caring for me.
Caring for me, is caring for me.

Copyright, 1886, by John J. Hood.

4 From yonder rainbow-circled throne,
   My Saviour is caring for me;
   Till I shall know as I am known,
   My Saviour is caring for me.

5 Oh, may I humbly serve him here!
   My Saviour is caring for me;
   And sing, when Jordan's waves appear,
   "My Saviour is caring for me."

72. A Better Day Coming On.

E. E. Hewitt.
Jno. R. Sweney.

1. There's a song of hope like a chime of bells, There's a better day coming on; And from year to year sweeter music swells Of the better day coming on.
2. All the pow'rs of sin shall in vain unite; There's a better day coming on; For the Word of God gives a promise bright, Of the better day coming on.
3. In the desert ways living streams shall flow, There's a better day coming on; And the heav'nly rose shall in beauty grow, There's a better day coming on.
4. Let us toil and trust, let us watch and pray, For the better day coming on; And the Lord himself will our work repay, In the better day coming on.

CHORUS.

There's a better day, There's a crowning day, There's a better day coming on; When the Lord our King Shall his glory bring, There's a better day coming on.

Copyright, 1892, by Jno. R. Sweney.

74. Precious Love.

T. E. T.
Rev. T. E. Terry.

1. Lord Jesus, thou knowest I love thee, And I know that thou lovest me; Thou wilt keep me for-ev-er se-curely, I am thine for e-ter-ni-ty.
2. While I walk thro' this val-ley of shadow, As-sault-ed by doubts and by fears, I know that my pathway is leading T'ward the land that has ne'er a tear.
3. And when the life-bat-tle is o-ver, I shall reign in thy kingdom with thee; Then I'll sing of sal-va-tion for-ev-er, And the King in his beau-ty see.
4. Then I'll sing of the love that redeem'd me, With the an-gels in glo-ry I'll sing, And all heaven shall ech-o the sto-ry— Halle-lu-jah to Christ our King.

CHORUS.

O the love of Christ from sin saves me, O bless the Lord, it saves! O the love of Christ from sin saves me, It saves forev-ermore.

O the love, precious love of Christ that saves from sin, all sin, saves me to-day, it saves! O the love, precious love of Christ that saves from sin, all sin, saves me to-day,

Copyright, 1878, by Jno. R. Sweney.

In God's Own Time.

Rev. Johnson Oatman, Jr.

"And let us not be weary in well doing: for in due season we shall reap, if we faint not."—Gal. vi: 9.

J. Howard Entwisle.

SOLO OR DUET

1. If o'er thy way dark clouds are cast, Look up with faith till they are past, The sun will surely shine at last, In God's own time, in God's own time.
2. Hast thou pray'd long and fervent-ly, And yet no an-swer came to thee? Thy pray'r will sometime answer'd be, In God's own time, in God's own time.
3. Look up with joy, nor long-er weep, Thy God will ev-'ry promise keep, And thou wilt yet the harvest reap, In God's own time, in God's own time.

CHORUS.

Then do not fear, tho' dark the night, But rise on wings of faith sublime,
Do not fear, tho' dark the night, rise on wings, on wings of faith sublime,

For ev'rything will come out right, In God's own time, in God's own time.
yes, ev'rything will come out right, in God's own time,

Copyright, 1896, by J. Howard Entwisle.

4 Tho' thro' the glass thou can'st not see,
And wonder why some things must be,
Yet thou wilt know each mystery,
In God's own time, in God's own time.

5 And would'st thou be forever blest?
Just trust in God and do thy best,
Then thou shalt enter into rest,
In God's own time, in God's own time.

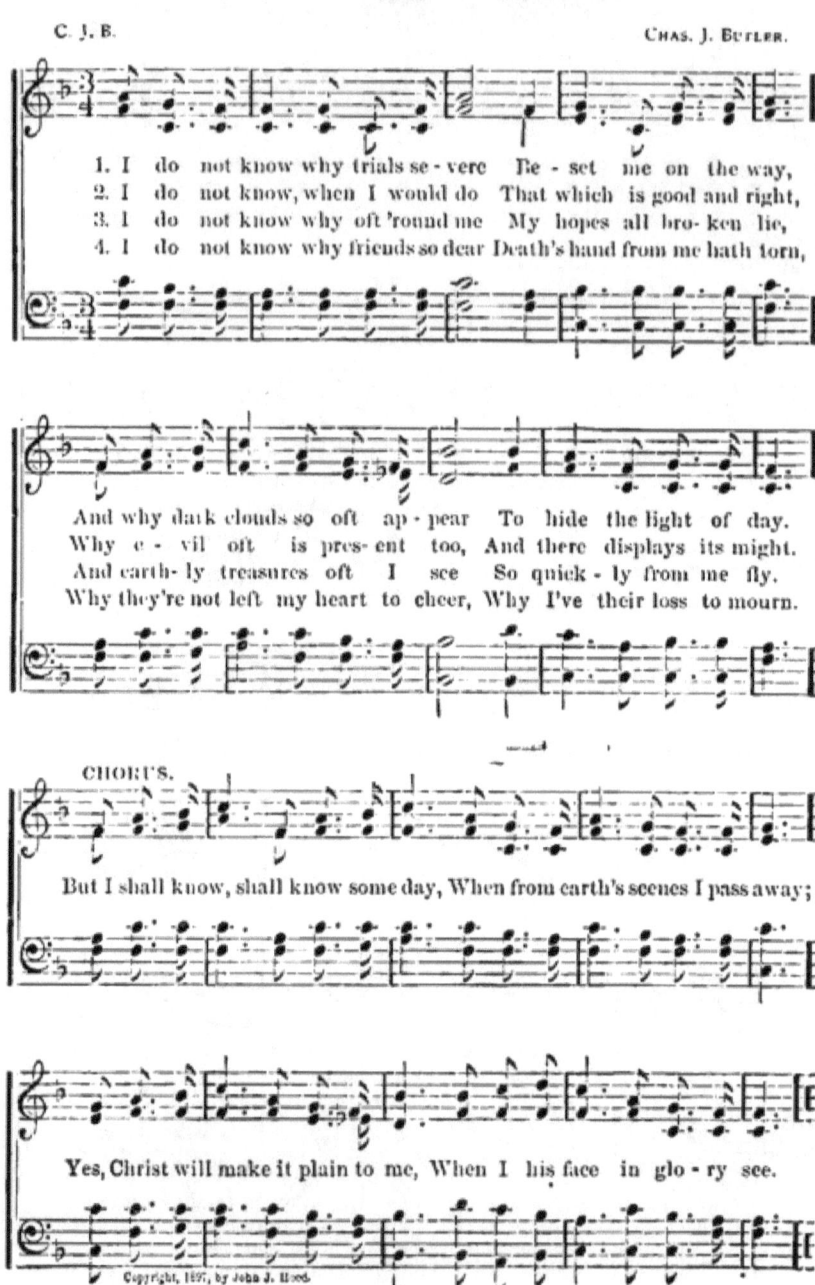

God's Three Hundred

Rev. Johnson Oatman, Jr. — Judges vii: 7. — Adam Geibel

1. Once, Gideon at God's command Took from his army great and grand A chosen few, a little band Of just three hundred; The rank and file, to their dismay, Were then discharg'd and sent away, But with the few he won the day, With those three hundred.

2. To-day we see church buildings stand In ev-'ry cit-y of our land, But in each fight God has a band, His own three hundred; Thro' rain or shine, thro' dark or light, These soldiers stand up for the right, And always win, tho' fierce the fight, God's own three hundred.

3. Oh, help us, Lord, to watch and pray, That we at last may hear thee say, "Well done, ye nobly won the day, My own three hundred;" Then, when there are no foes to fight, In that blest land where comes no night, O may we walk with thee in white, Thy sav'd three hundred.

CHORUS.
The brave three hundred, The Lord's three hundred; O help us, Lord, to number'd be With thy three hundred.

Copyright, 1898, by J. Howard Entwisle.

82. He hath Set His Love upon Me.

Rev. Johnson Oatman, Jr.   J. Howard Entwisle.

1. He hath set his love up-on me, oh, how precious is the seal,
2. He hath set his love up-on me, tho' de-filed and born in sin,
3. He hath set his love up-on me, and hath call'd me thus his own,
4. He hath set his love up-on me, I am his for life or death,

Oh, what ho-ly ben-e-dictions ev-er in my heart I feel!
Yet the bless-ed Saviour sought me, and his strong arm took me in;
And his pres-ence doth go with me, for I nev-er walk a-lone;
And I know he'll stand be-side me when I draw my clos-ing breath;

For it brings me greater blessings than my spir-it can contain, He hath
For I heard his sweet voice calling, "child, come unto me and rest," He hath
Tho' the way leads over mountains, or thro' valleys dark and deep, He hath
Then with-in the walls of jas-per, when I reach that land so fair, He hath

rit.   **CHORUS.**

set his love upon me, blessed be his ho-ly name. He hath set his love up-
set his love upon me, and I lean up-on his breast.
set his love upon me, and his child he'll safely keep.
set his love upon me, and I know he'll own me there.

on me, oh, the blessed, blessed seal! He hath set his love up-on me, when him-

Copyright, 1898, by John J. Hood.

4 Let earnest pray'rs to God ascend,
   And on his word if we depend,
   The heav'nly fire shall then descend,
      As in the days of old.

5 Come, Holy Spirit, thou who art
   Willing to touch with fire the heart,
   Thy sacred light and warmth impart,
      As in the days of old.

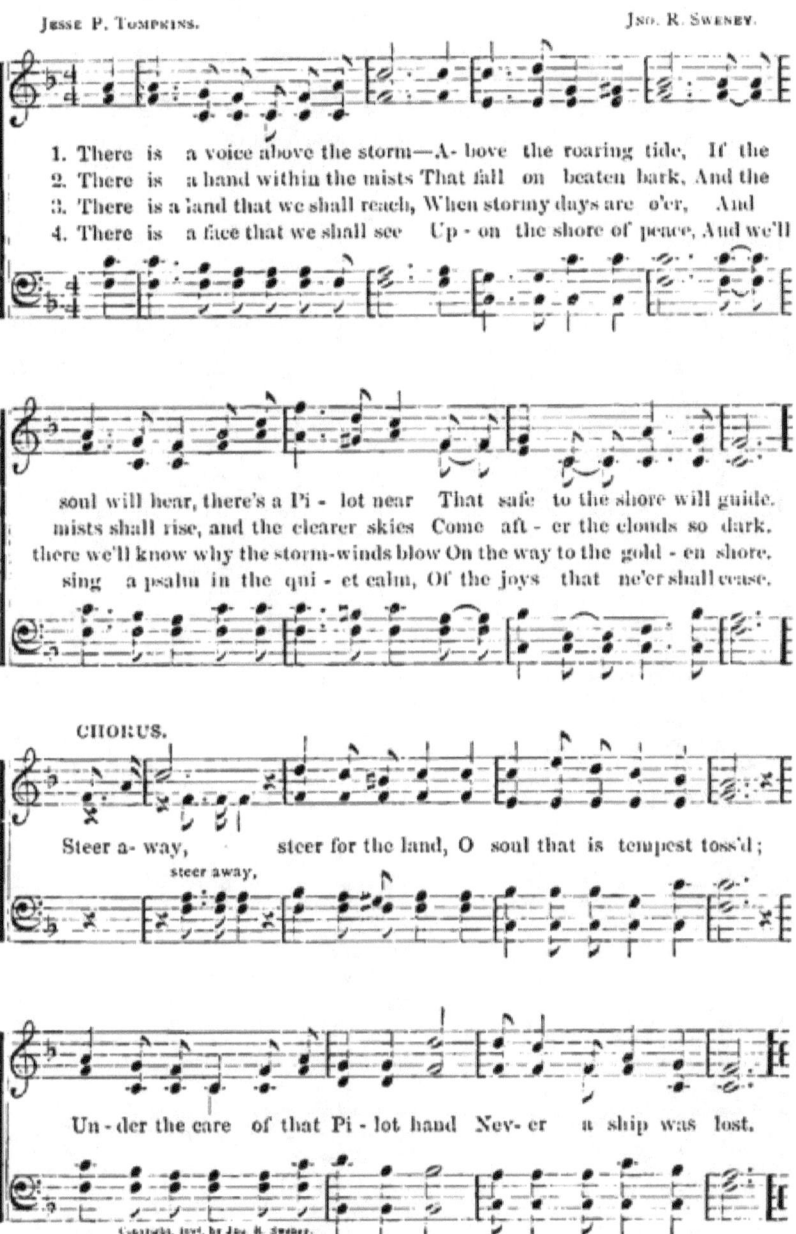

Lean On Jesus and Rest.

Rev. Johnson Oatman, Jr. J. Howard Entwisle.

1. Like as a bird at eve-ning Flies to its mountain nest,
2. When with life's work I'm burdened, When with life's cares I'm pressed,
3. E'en tho' I walk thro' sor-row, Knowing his will is best,

So may my heart when wea-ry Lean on Je-sus and rest. . . .
Soft-ly there comes a whisper, "Lean on Je-sus and rest." . . .
I will without a murmur Lean on Je-sus and rest.

and rest.

CHORUS.

Lean on Je-sus and rest, . . . Lean on Je-sus and rest: . . . .
sweet rest, precious rest;

O soul, so burden'd and wea-ry, Lean on Je-sus and rest.

Copyright, 1896, by John J. Hood.

4 No spot on earth so precious,
No place on earth so blest,
As, when I—nothing doubting—
Lean on Jesus and rest.

5 And when at last life's sunset
Lights up the golden west,
Then will my soul forever
Lean on Jesus and rest.

88. Come, Brother, and Join with Me.

H. E. S.
Howard E. Smith.

1. My sins I've laid at Jesus' feet, Come, brother, and join with me;
2. I have a friend, a friend indeed, Come, brother, and join with me;
3. I'll join the lov'd ones o-ver there, Come, brother, and join with me;
4. Unsaved one, now the Saviour meet, Come, brother, and join with me;

I've found a rest so pure and sweet, Come, brother, and join with me.
Who ne'er will leave in time of need, Come, brother, and join with me.
In yonder home so bright and fair, Come, brother, and join with me.
There's pardon at the mer-cy-seat, Come, brother, and join with me.

CHORUS.

Come, brother, and join with me, . . . Come, brother, and join with me; . . .
  and join with me,   and join with me;

I've found a rest so pure and sweet, Come, brother, and join with me.

Copyright, 1892, by John J. Hood.

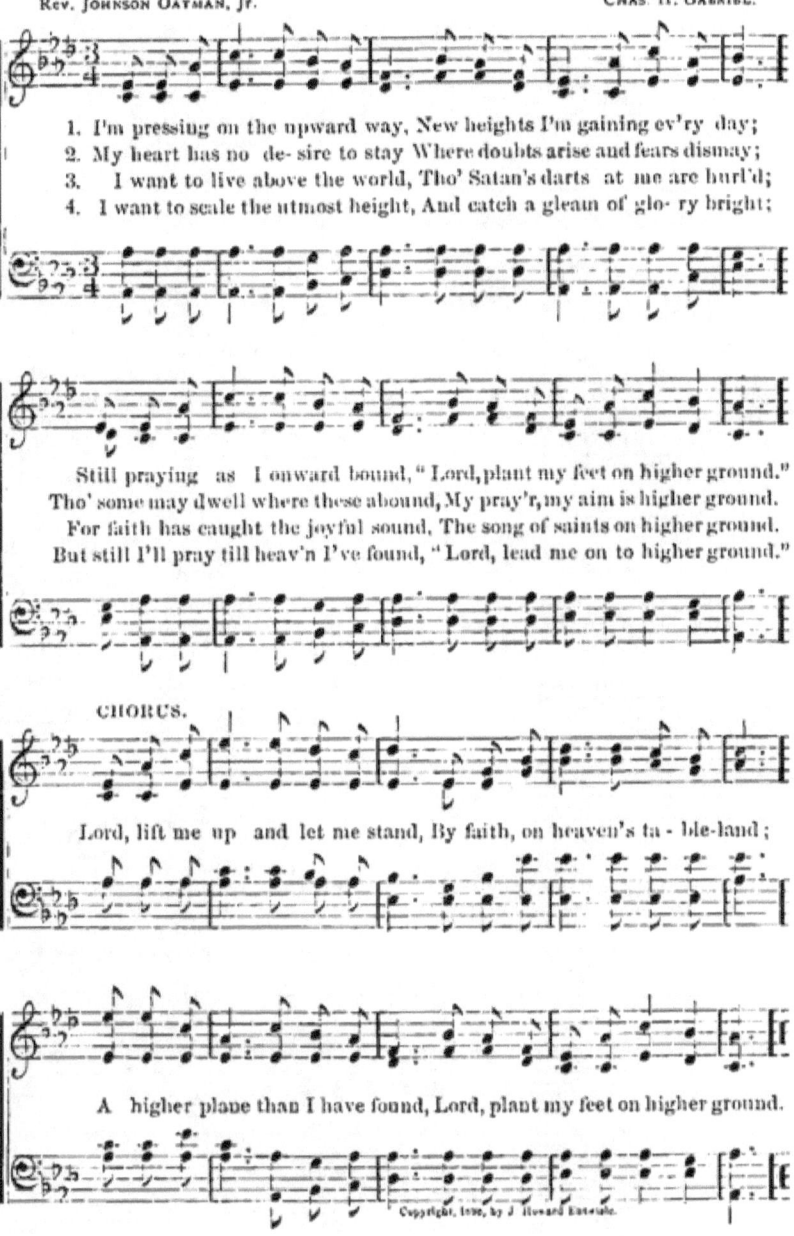

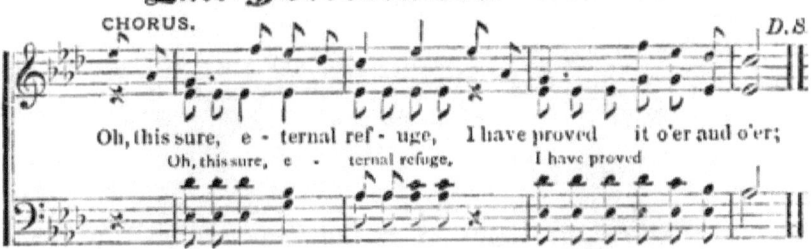

CHORUS.
D.S.
Oh, this sure, e - ternal ref - uge, I have proved it o'er and o'er;
Oh, this sure, e - ternal refuge, I have proved

He Pays Me Right Along.

Rev. Johnson Oatman, Jr. J. Howard Entwisle.

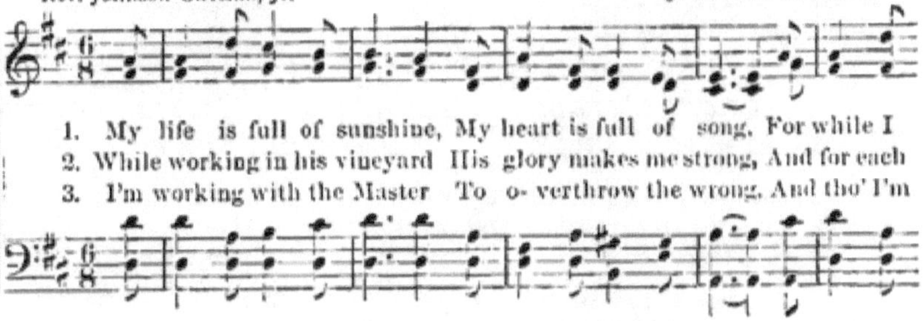
1. My life is full of sunshine, My heart is full of song, For while I
2. While working in his vineyard His glory makes me strong, And for each
3. I'm working with the Master To o- verthrow the wrong, And tho' I'm

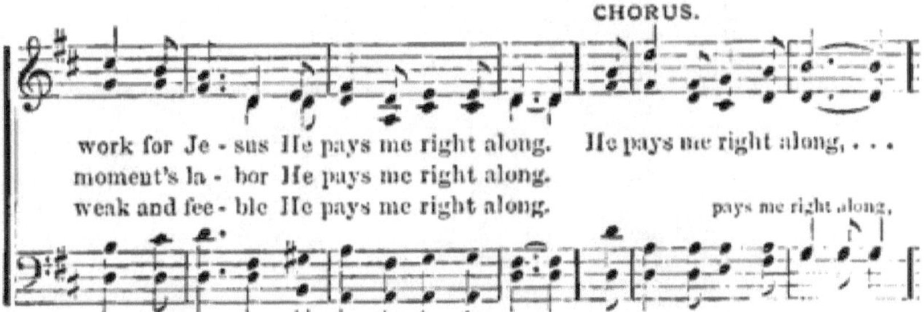
CHORUS.
work for Je - sus He pays me right along. He pays me right along, . . .
moment's la - bor He pays me right along.
weak and fee - ble He pays me right along.
pays me right along,

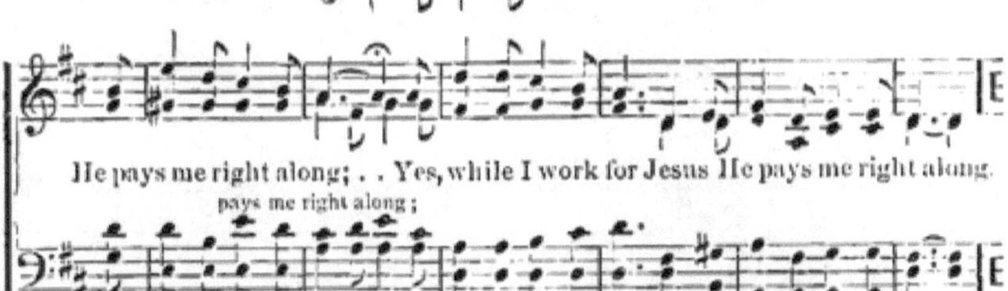
He pays me right along; . . Yes, while I work for Jesus He pays me right along.
pays me right along;

4 Until I reach the Jordan,
His praise I will prolong;
For he's the best of Masters,
He pays me right along.

5 I know I'll get to heaven,
And join the blood-washed throng,
But while I'm on the journey
He pays me right along.

The Penitent's Plea.—CONCLUDED.

sin away, Pow'r to keep me sinless day by day, For me, for me!
sin a-way, Pow'r to keep me sin-less day by day, For me, for me, for me!

Are You Sowing for the Master?

IDA L. REED. JNO. R. SWENEY.

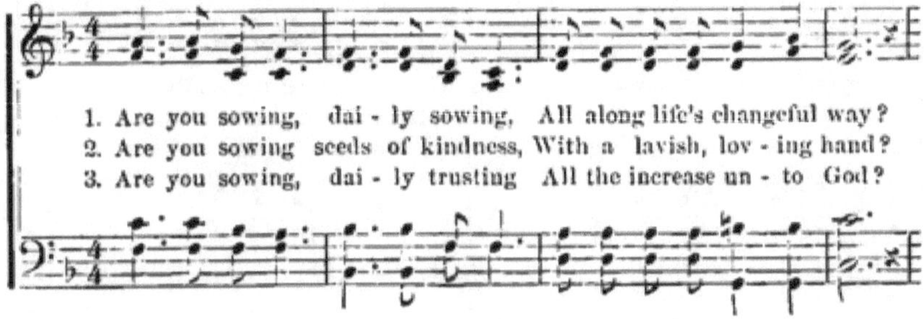

1. Are you sowing, dai-ly sowing, All along life's changeful way?
2. Are you sowing seeds of kindness, With a lavish, lov-ing hand?
3. Are you sowing, dai-ly trusting All the increase un-to God?

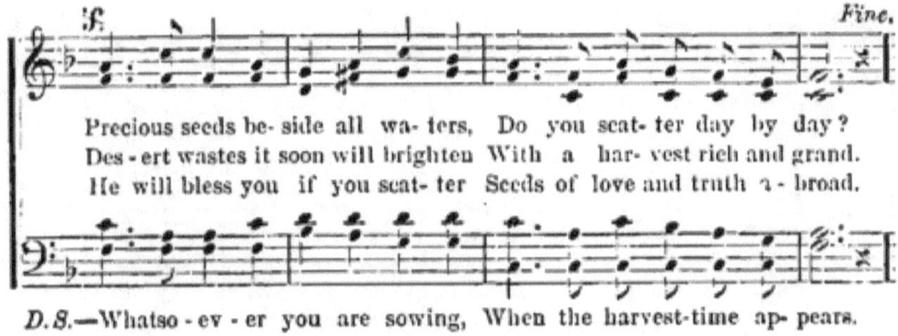

Precious seeds be-side all wa-ters, Do you scat-ter day by day?
Des-ert wastes it soon will brighten With a har-vest rich and grand.
He will bless you if you scat-ter Seeds of love and truth a-broad.

D.S.—Whatso-ev-er you are sowing, When the harvest-time ap-pears.

CHORUS.

Are you sowing for the Master? You shall reap in joy or tears

Copyright, 1896, by Jno. R. Sweney.

Love and Praise, No. 5.—G

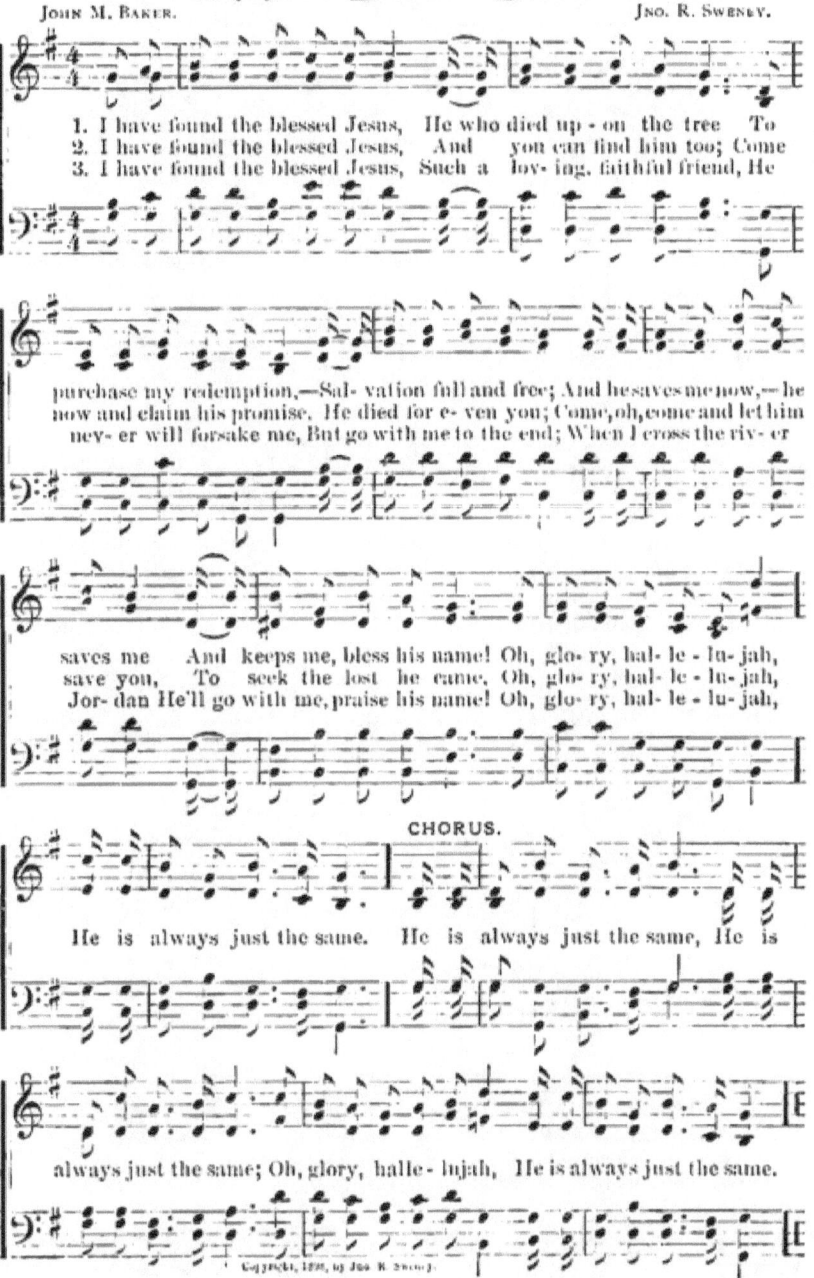

The Good Shepherd.

Words arr. by J. H. E.
J. Howard Entwisle

1. The snow was drifting o'er the hills, The wind was fierce and loud,
2. "I saw thy flock at peace within Thine own well-guarded fold;
3. "But since thy flock are all secure, Why to the height repair?

While forward press'd the Shepherd Good, His head in sorrow bowed:
O Shepherd, pause, for wild the gale That rages o'er the world!"
If thou hast ninety-nine at home, Why for a truant care?"

"O Shepherd, rest, nor farther go, The tempest hath begun."
"No; one poor lamb hath gone astray, And soon may be undone;
"Dearer to me than all the rest Is that poor, struggling son!

I cannot stay, I must away To seek my little one!"
I cannot stay, I must away To seek my little one!"
I cannot stay, I must away To seek my little one!"

Copyright, 1898, by John J. Hood.

4 "Good Shepherd, tell me, if his need
Should bring the wanderer home,
Wilt thou not punish him with stripes,
Lest he again should roam?"
"No; I would clasp him to my heart,
As mother clasps her son,
I cannot stay, I must away
To seek my little one!"

5 E'en so, I thought, our gracious Lord
Hath in his heart divine
A wealth of love for all his saints—
For all the ninety-nine!
But most he loves, and most he seeks
The soul by sin undone;
And still he sighs, "I must away
To seek my little one!"

When Life is Ended.—CONCLUDED. 105

I may share it with some dear one I have help'd to lead to thee.
I may share it with some dear one I have help'd to lead, to lead to thee.

O Wondrous Cross.

E. E. Hewitt.   Jno. R. Sweney.

1. My Saviour bore the curse for me, Glad praises will I give, To him whose
2. The blood that takes my sins away, Ten thousand joys will bring; New strength for
3. His Spirit, sent from heav'n above, Bears witness with my soul; While billows
4. O mighty stream! so deep, so broad, It fills my heart with peace; The blood hath

CHORUS.

blood hath made me free, Who died that I might live. O won - drous cross! O
service ev'ry day, New songs for me to sing.
of redeeming love, Still down from Calv'ry roll.
brought me nigh to God, Ne'er shall my praises cease. O wondrous, wondrous cross! O

pre - cious blood! He died that I might live; All glory be to God.
precious, precious blood!   glo - ry be to God.

Copyright, 1893, by Jno. R. Sweney.

Seeking the Lost.—CONCLUDED.

Nothing but Mercy for Me.

Mrs. Frank A. Breck.   J. Howard Entwisle.

1. My blest Redeemer left heaven one day, From sin to make me free—
2. My Lord was willing to suf-fer and die, To bring me lib-er-ty,
3. My Lord and Saviour is liv-ing a-gain, At God's right hand to be,

He took my grief and guilt a-way, And so there is mer-cy for me.
My sin-ful soul to pur-i-fy, And so there is mer-cy for me.
And there he lives to plead for men, And so there is mer-cy for me.

CHORUS.

Oh, wonderful, wonderful mercy of God, As deep as the boundless sea!
His blood was spilt to cleanse my guilt, And there's nothing but mercy for me.

Copyright, 1896, by John J. Hood.

Fill to Overflowing.—CONCLUDED. 111

flowing; Fill me now, .. fill me now, With thy Holy Spir-it, Lord.
Fill me now, fill me now,

Full and Free.

Rev. JOHNSON OATMAN, Jr.   J. HOWARD ENTWISLE.

1. When Je-sus died on Calv'ry's tree, He bought SALVATION full and free;
2. When blind with sin, I could not see, He brought his MERCY full and free;
3. Yes, Je-sus is so good to me, His LOVE he giv-eth full and free;
4. And when I reach e-ter-ni-ty, I'll find a WELCOME full and free;

For me he made the sac-ri-fice, For me he paid the fear-ful price.
He shed on me his beams of light, And my blind eyes received their sight.
He guides me all a-long life's way, He watches o'er me night and day.
He'll put on me a robe and crown, And I will by his side sit down.

D.S.—full and free, Hosan-na, bless his ho-ly name!

CHORUS.

Full and free, full and free, The blood of Jesus cleanseth me; 'Tis full and free,

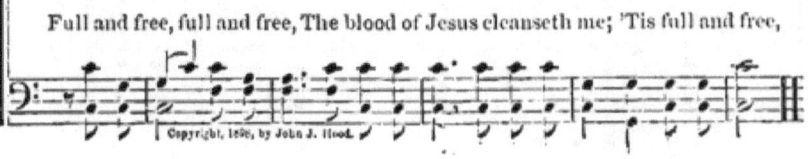

Copyright, 1896, by John J. Hood.

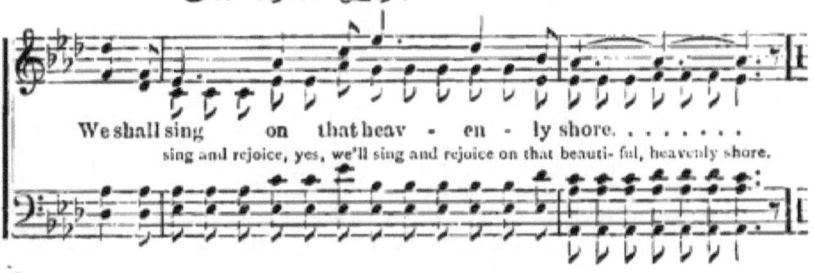

Lost After All.

Rev. Johnson Oatman, Jr.   J. Howard Entwisle.

1. 'Tis sad to think, that tho' some hear So many times, year af-ter year,
2. The Saviour says, "come un-to me, I'll save your soul, I'll set you free,"
3. Dear friends are in the land so fair, Perhaps they bade you meet them there,

The bless-ed gos-pel call,—God's love they spurn from day to day, Un-
Oh, hear him sweetly call; Then, sin-ner, come, no long-er wait,—To-
Your promise now re-call; They're watching for you down life's way, Oh,

til at last the an-gels say, "Lost af-ter all, lost af-ter all!"
morrow it may be too late,— Lost af-ter all, lost af-ter all!
will they ev-er have to say, "Lost af-ter all, lost af-ter all?"

Copyright, 1896, by J. Howard Entwisle.

4 Salvation why will you neglect?
Why longer still do you reject
The Holy Spirit's call?
Oh, let it not of you be said
These words so sad, when you are dead,
"Lost after all, lost after all!"

5 Then come to Jesus, come just now,
Low at his footstool humbly bow,
He'll hear you when you call;
Shall angels bear the joyful news?
Or must they say, if you refuse,
"Lost after all, lost after all?"

Love and Praise, No. 5—H

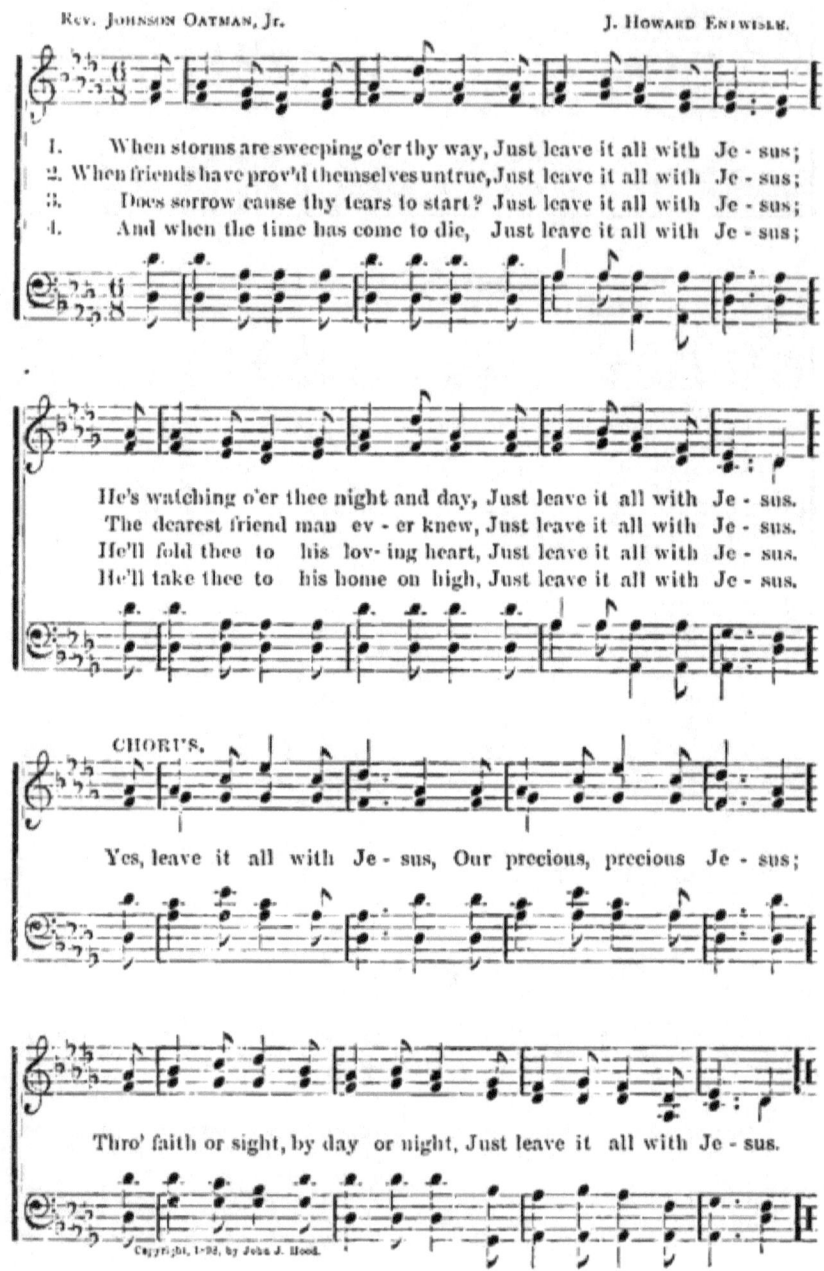

He Loveth My Soul.—CONCLUDED.

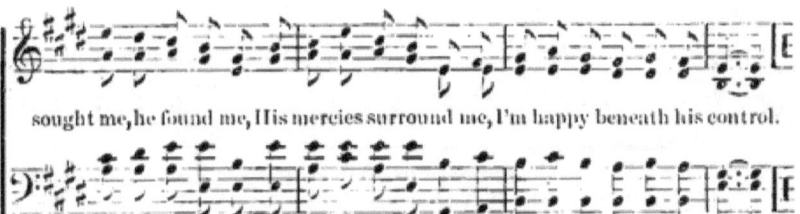

sought me, he found me, His mercies surround me, I'm happy beneath his control.

Bethany's Comforter.

JESSE P. TOMPKINS.   CHAS. BENTLEY.

1. Bethany's Comforter comes to bless In the dark hour of deep distress;
2. Bethany's Comforter weeps with me, O- ver the faces I can- not see,
3. Bethany's Comforter brings a balm, Lo! on my spirit there falls a calm;
4. Bethany's Comforter I shall see When in the dawning the mists shall flee;

When in my sorrow his face I see, Then all the darkening shadows flee.
Tenderly touches my pain and grief, Bringing the promise of sweet relief.
When in life's tempest he whispers, "peace," Oh, how the turbulent billows cease.
In that bright morning beyond the gloom I shall have victo- ry o'er the tomb.

D.S.—Sunshine or shadow, whatever it be, Bethany's Comforter cometh to me.

CHORUS.   D.S.

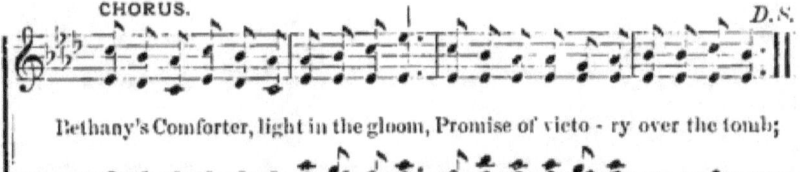

Bethany's Comforter, light in the gloom, Promise of victo - ry over the tomb;

Copyright, 1887, by John J. Hood.

Open the Door for Me.

Rev. Johnson Oatman, Jr.
Jno. R. Sweney.

1. When darkness is hedging my way,—The path I no long-er can see,
2. When danger would threaten my soul, "To whom can I go but to thee?"
3. Within thy dear church here below, Of use to thee, Master, I'd be;
4. And when at the pearl gate I knock, De-siring ad-mission to thee,

I go to my clos-et and pray, "Lord, o-pen the door for me."
When billows would o-ver me roll, Lord, o-pen the door for me.
Oh, show me just where I should go,— Lord, o-pen the door for me.
Oh, bid those fair portals un-lock,—Lord, o-pen the door for me.

CHORUS.

O-pen the door, o-pen the door; Oh, bid all the shadows flee;

O-pen the door, open the door,—Lord, o-pen the door for me.

Copyright, 1895, by Jno. R. Sweney.

Living for Jesus Only. 119

Rev. J. G. Bickerton.   Edwin S. Gault.

1. Living for Jesus meekly each day; Fill'd with his fulness, O joyful lay!
2. Blessings he gives me, precious and sweet, Strengthens my faith for vict'ry complete;
3. O wondrous grace, O power divine, That we should in thy blest image shine
4. In realms of glory, thy face to see, Join'd with the ransom'd all about thee,

This is life's sto-ry with Christ alway, Living for Je-sus on-ly.
Safe-ly I'm kept at Je-sus' feet, Living for Je-sus on-ly.
And live sustain'd by pow'r wholly thine, Living for Je-sus on-ly.
Then we will praise thee in ho-ly glee, Living for Je-sus on-ly.

CHORUS.

Living for Je-sus all the day long, Singing for Je-sus, that is my song;
Fighting the battle of right against wrong, Living for Je-sus on-ly.

Copyright, 1899, by J. Howard Entwisle.

I've a Blessing every Day.

J. B. MACKAY.   W. T. DASHIELL.

1. I've a blessing ev-'ry day, Since I started on the way To the
2. All my ransom'd pow'rs combin'd To my Saviour I've resign'd, I am
3. I am climbing to the height Where the sun is always bright, I have

blessed, blessed land of light a-bove, (above,) And al-tho' my life was sweet,
happy, for I know that he is near; (is near;) I shall never be dismay'd,
left the mist-y val-ley far be-low; (below:) I believe there's light untold,

Still I found it incomplete, Till the Saviour fill'd my soul with perfect love.
For my hope on him is stay'd, And his perfect love has banish'd all my fear.
That my eyes shall yet behold, For the way is growing brighter as I go.

D.S.—blessed Lord divine Fill'd my soul all thro' and thro' with perfect love.

CHORUS.

Perfect love,   perfect love.   'Tis the best of all the
Perfect love,   perfect love,

gra-ces from a-bove; Wondrous peace and joy are mine, Since the
a-bove;

Copyright, 1893, by Jno. R. Sweney.

Joy and Sunshine.

123

Mary Marsh.
Jno. R. Sweney.

1. Jesus is my joy and sunshine, All along life's dreary way;
   His blest presence makes my pathway Bright as heaven's golden day.
2. And the glory of his presence Fills my weary soul with peace;
   And my heart is full of gladness—Full of songs that nev-er cease.
3. Day by day the way grows brighter; O'er my path heav'ns golden ray
   Sheds its beams of glorious sunlight, Like un-to the "perfect day."
4. Beauties never seen by mor-tals, To the eye of faith appears;
   As we near the heav'nly portals, Far beyond this vale of tears.

CHORUS.

Joy, joy, blessed joy and sunshine, Fills my happy soul to-day; . . . . .
my happy soul to-day;
Peace, blessed peace is ev-er mine, Shining all a-long my way.

Copyright, 1876, by Jno. R. Sweney.

124 Happy All the Day.

Rev. Johnson Oatman, Jr. J. Howard Entwisle.

1. Once I was heavy la-den, Borne down with sin and woe, I cried out
2. No more my way is drear-y, My heart is full of spring, No time for
3. My life is full of sunshine, My soul is full of love, I'm on my
4. Some day I'll reach the cit-y Where my fair mansion stands, And there en-

"who will help me, Ah, whither shall I go?" I heard a sweet voice
dull re-pin-ing, For now I shout and sing; I'm glad I sought his
way to heav-en, That gold-en land a-bove; I'm glad I ev-er
joy for-ev-er "That house not made with hands;" But while my blessed

an-swer, "I am the Life, the Way," And since I turned to Je-sus
fa-vor, I'm glad I learned to pray, For since I've been forgiv-en
en-tered The straight and narrow way, For here I find such glo-ry,
Saviour, Is with me on the way, It seems so much like heaven,

CHORUS.

I'm happy all the day, I'm happy all the day, I'm happy
hap-py all the day,

all the way; Yes, since I found my Saviour I'm happy all the day.
hap-py all the way;

Copyright, 1898, by J. Howard Entwisle.

The Saviour Walks Beside Me.

125

C. B.
CHAS. BENTLEY.

1. I never weary trav'ling the way my Father's trod, The Saviour walks be-
2. Whilst climbing hills and mountains I never shall despair, The Saviour walks be-
3. 'Mid tri- als and temptations my journey I pursue, The Saviour walks be-
4. I know that all my troubles and trav'ling soon will cease, The Saviour walks be-

side me ev-'ry day; I gain from him fresh courage by trusting in his word,
side me ev-'ry day; I have his precious promise "my child, you need not fear,"
side me ev-'ry day; He cheers me with a whisper, my strength he doth renew,
side me ev-'ry day; And I shall live for- ev- er with him in perfect peace,

Fine. CHORUS.

The Saviour walks beside me all the way. The Saviour walks beside me, he

D. S.—Saviour walks beside me all the way.

comforts and he guides me, He strengthens and he keeps me ev'ry day;

D. S.

No e- vil shall be- tide me, he'll safe- ly, safe- ly hide me, The

Copyright, 1877, by John J. Hood.

126. When I Hear the Trumpet Sounding.

Jno. R. Clements. 1 Cor. xv: 52; Matt. xxiv: 31; 1 Thess. iv: 16. Jno. R. Sweney.

1. When I hear the trumpet sounding that shall call forth from their rest, All those sleeping in the quiet of the tomb; I'll be glad to hear the summons, with the Lord to go and reign, In a land where never enters death nor gloom.
2. If that note shall break the stillness in the quiet hours of night, Or it soundeth in the busy heat of day; Those asleep in Christ will answer, those awake caught up will be, And togeth-er all with him will speed away.
3. In that land is naught of sorrow, there is music ev'rywhere, There is nothing that is in the minor key; But the sweetest songs and anthems there they swell with heart and voice, 'Tis a land of one un-ending ju-bi-lee.

CHORUS.

When I hear...... the trumpet sound---ing, When I hear..... the trumpet sounding.... When I hear... the trumpet
When I hear the trumpet sounding, trumpet sounding, When I hear the trumpet sounding, trumpet sounding, When I hear the trumpet

Copyright, 1890, by Jno. R. Sweney.

When I Hear, etc.—CONCLUDED.

sound - ing, I'll be glad with Christ to quickly take my way. . . .
sounding, trumpet sounding,   take my way

Hosanna! Bless His Name.

Rev. JOHNSON OATMAN, Jr.   J. HOWARD ENTWISLE.

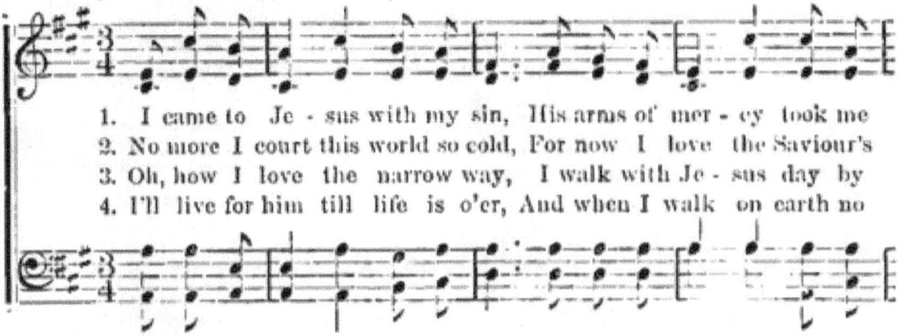

1. I came to Je - sus with my sin, His arms of mer - cy took me
2. No more I court this world so cold, For now I love the Saviour's
3. Oh, how I love the narrow way, I walk with Je - sus day by
4. I'll live for him till life is o'er, And when I walk on earth no

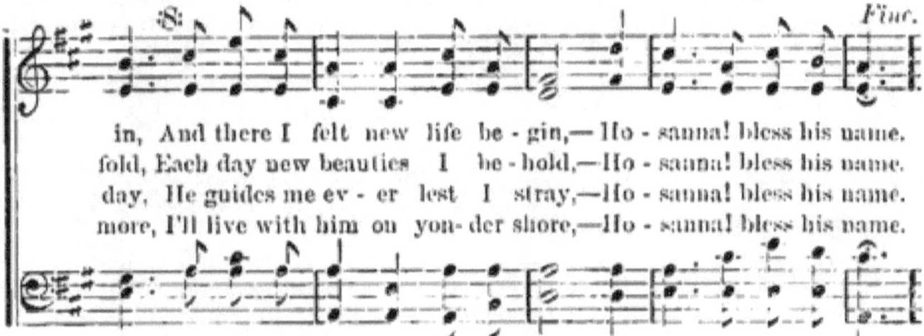

in, And there I felt new life be - gin,—Ho - sanna! bless his name.
fold, Each day new beauties I be - hold,—Ho - sanna! bless his name.
day, He guides me ev - er lest I stray,—Ho - sanna! bless his name.
more, I'll live with him on yon - der shore,—Ho - sanna! bless his name.

D.S.—He took a - way my guilt and shame,—Ho - sanna! bless his name.

CHORUS.   D.S.

O bless his name, O bless his name, To me the Lord of glo - ry came,

Copyright, 1896, by John J. Lloyd.

Jesus, the Light, etc.—CONCLUDED. 129

I will confess him, And worship and bless him, The beautiful Light of my soul!
beautiful Light of my soul!

O Come Just Now.

Rev. JOHNSON OATMAN, Jr.   JNO. R. SWENEY.

1. Come, sinner, to the Saviour, Now seek his face and fa-vor, Why do you long-er waver? O come just now.
2. God's servants are ap-pealing, The moments fast are stealing, O do not wait for feeling, But come just now.
3. Pray'rs are for you as-cending, E-ter-nal doom is pending, O'er you are angels bending, O come just now.

CHORUS.

O come just now, O come just now, O come just now, While Jesus waits to save you, O come just now.
O come just now, O come just now, O come, O come just now.

Copyright, 1898, by Jno. R. Sweney.

4 Come with thy sin and sorrow,
  Time is not yours to borrow,
  O wait not for the morrow,
    But come just now.

5 The Spirit long has striven,
  O come and be forgiven,
  Come, start for home and heaven,
    And come just now.

Love and Praise, No. 5,—1

130. Waiting at the Mercy Seat.

Mrs. C. H. M.   Mrs. C. H. Morris.

1. Father, thou art willing to bestow The Spirit's pow'r upon thy children;
2. Search me, Lord, and know this heart of mine, Have I surrender'd to thee fully?
3. As the branches of the Living Vine, Are we, thy children, now abiding?

And we cannot, cannot let thee go Until the precious boon is giv-en.
Is my will completely lost in thine, The Spirit's dwelling place made holy?
May we claim the promis'd pow'r divine To all who come in faith confiding.

REFRAIN.

Waiting at the mer-cy seat, O Father, We are waiting at the mer-cy seat; For the Spirit's pow'r and blessing, Waiting at the mercy seat.

Copyright, 1898, by John J. Hood.

4 Bid us not go hence nor leave thy throne,
   Until thy Spirit thou'rt bestowing;
Till in us thy perfect will be done,
   And all the fullness we are knowing.

5 Hush'd the raging tempest in my soul,
   As Christ to peace the storm is stilling;
Waves of comfort now above me roll,
   As he with love my soul is filling.

Where Wilt Thou Land?

131

The last words of Pilot Millard F. Lindle, of Camden, N. J., were: "Beautiful! Where shall we land?——Here we are; we're landed!"

Rev. WILLIAM H. BANCROFT. JNO. R SWENEY.

DUET.

1. Sail-ing down the stream of time, Bound for death's expand-ed sea,
2. Soon will heave that sea in sight, Then the landing will ap-pear;
3. Wouldst thou, sinner, at thy death, Have ce-les-tial visions bright,
4. Je-sus let thy pi-lot be, Safe he'll guide a-cross the wave;

Sinner, will a bet-ter clime Scenes of grandeur bring to thee?
Will it be a port of light, Or a wast-ed place and drear?
And breathe out thy parting breath With a dy-ing saint's delight?
He's the Mas-ter of the sea, He will land thee, he will save.

CHORUS.

Where, O sin-ner, wilt thou land, When life's voy-age all is o'er?
Where, O sinner, When life's voyage

Wilt thou reach ... the golden strand Of a fair-er, brighter shore?
Wilt thou reach   golden strand   Of a fairer, brighter shore?

Copyright, 1888, by Jno. R. Sweney.

134. What Shall Our Record Be?

F. M. D. — SOLO AND CHORUS. — Frank M. Davis.

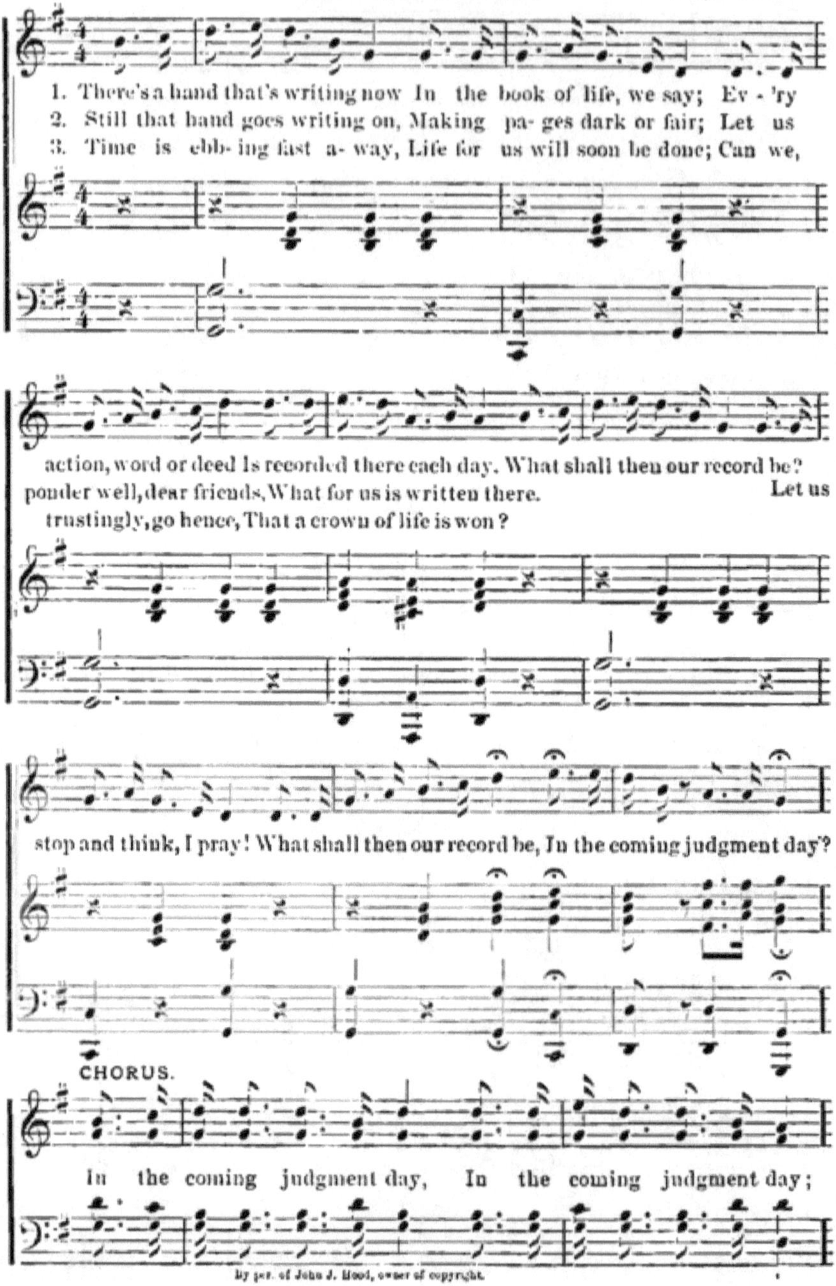

1. There's a hand that's writing now In the book of life, we say; Ev-'ry action, word or deed Is recorded there each day. What shall then our record be?
2. Still that hand goes writing on, Making pa-ges dark or fair; Let us ponder well, dear friends, What for us is written there.
3. Time is ebb-ing fast a-way, Life for us will soon be done; Can we trustingly, go hence, That a crown of life is won?

Let us stop and think, I pray! What shall then our record be, In the coming judgment day?

CHORUS.

In the coming judgment day, In the coming judgment day;

by per. of John J. Hood, owner of copyright.

Living Water.

Jesse P. Tompkins. Jno. R. Sweney.

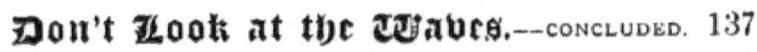

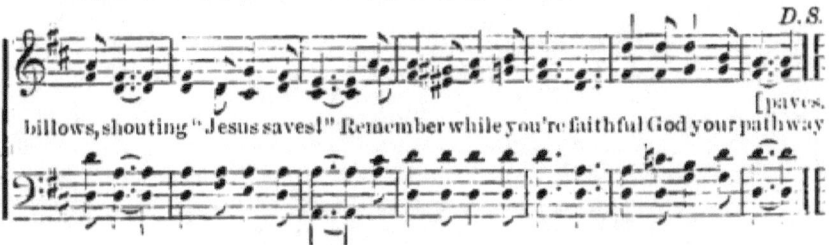

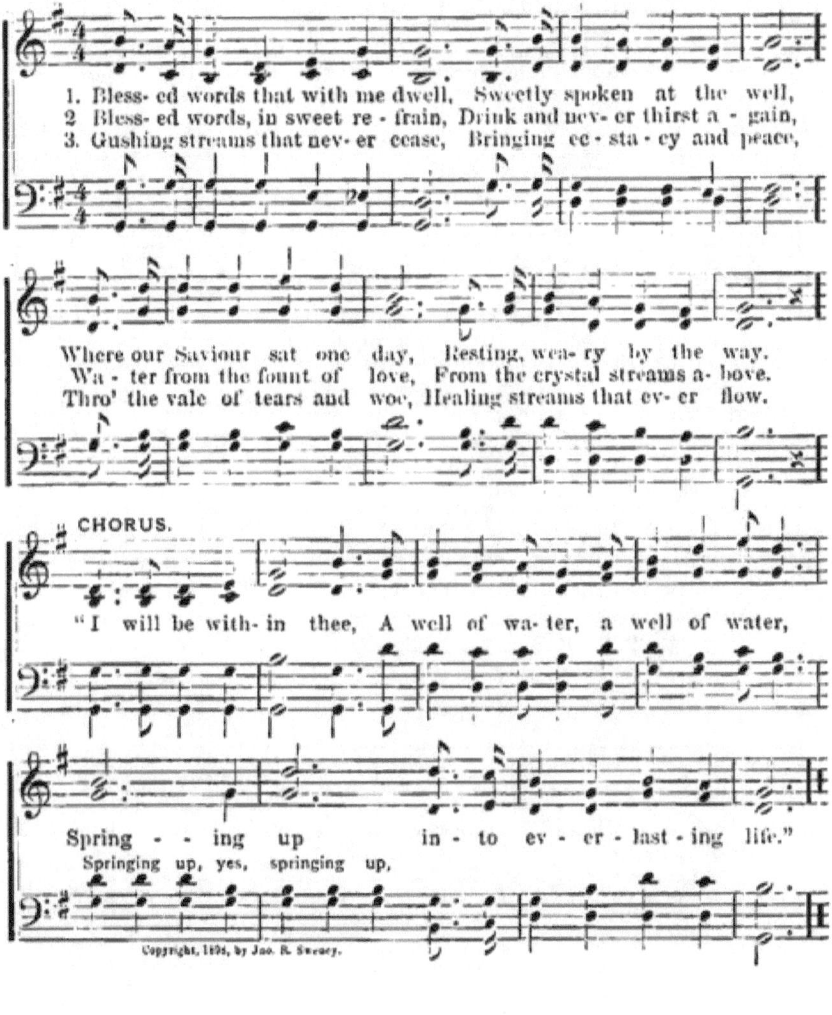

The Heights of Beulah Land.

HARRIET E. JONES. J. HOWARD ENTWISLE.

1. I am dwelling with my Saviour on the heights of Beulah land, And he
2. In the presence of my Saviour there is joy and sweet content, And I
3. Guided by my blessed Saviour I will reach the gate a-jar, That shall

holds me in his tender love and care; Thro' the pleasant paths he leads me, With the
love his blest commandments to obey; With this tender Friend beside me, Ev'ry
lead me to the Christian's final goal; Then with him who kindly sought me, And whose

D.S.—pass the pearly portal, To the

Fine.

bread of life he feeds me, As we journey t'ward that City, bright and fair.
hour to love and guide me, Brighter grows the Christian pathway, day by day.
precious blood has bought me, I will live while blissful a-ges onward roll.

shining home immortal, Ev-ermore to dwell with Jesus on the right.

CHORUS. D.S.

In communion with my Saviour, With the Cit-y just in sight; Soon I'll

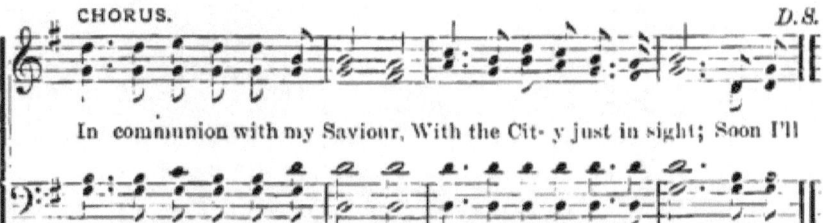

Copyright, 1893, by John J. Hood.

I'll Go where You, etc.—CONCLUDED. 149

I'll say what you want me to say, dear Lord, I'll be what you want me to be.

Don't You Know He Cares?

Like Elijah, when he sat under the Juniper tree and prayed for the Lord to take his life, how often we in hours of trouble, sit under our Juniper tree of sorrow alone and cry out, "I am passing through the waters and 'Nobody Cares.'"

Rev. JOHNSON OATMAN, Jr.   J. HOWARD ENTWISLE

1. When your spirit bows in sor-row From the load it bears, Go and
2. Have your feet become entan-gled In the tempter's snares? There is
3. Have you been by grief o'ertak-en, Stricken un-awares? Yet you
4. Is your body fill'd with anguish, With the pain it bears? Think of

Fine. **CHORUS.**

tell your heart to Jesus,—Don't you know he cares? Yes, there is One who
One who died to save you, Don't you know he cares?
will not be for-sak-en, Don't you know he cares?
how the Saviour suffered—Don't you know he cares?

D.S.—Don't you know he cares?

D.S.

shares your burdens, Ev'ry sorrow shares; Go and tell it all to Je-sus,—

Copyright 1897, by John J. Hood.

5. Loss of friends and loss of fortune—
Life a dark look wears;
Yet the Saviour still is with you,
Don't you know he cares?

6. So amid life's cares and struggles,
Blending songs with prayers—
Always put your trust in Jesus,
Don't you know he cares?

150. The Harbor Lights of Home.

Mrs. Ida M. Budd.
Chas. H. Gabriel.

1. O'er the trackless deep the sail-or sails for many a wea-ry day,
2. O'er life's sea the Christian sail-or steers his bark with stead-y hand,
3. So when fair skies bend above us, as we glide the bil-lows o'er,

Long-ing for the peace-ful ha-ven and the dear ones far a-way;
Knowing that his chart and compass will di-rect him safe to land;
Or when dark'ning shadows gath-er, and the tempests rage and roar,

But he keeps his heart with courage as his good ship parts the foam,
And he finds a calm in tu-mult, and a brightness in the gloom,
We will trust that to the ha-ven of our hopes we soon shall come,

For he knows that in the distance shine the har-bor lights of home.
As his face beholds the shin-ing of the har-bor lights of home.
Guid-ed by the stead-y gleaming of the har-bor lights of home.

CHORUS.

The home lights are shining! The home lights are shining! Bright-ly
Brightly beaming

Copyright, 1896, by Chas. H. Gabriel. John J. Hood, owner.

The Harbor Lights, etc.—CONCLUDED. 151

beaming ev-ermore; .... Tho' they sometimes gleam but faintly thro' the
brightly beaming, beaming evermore;

mist that veils the shore, Yet we know they are shining, shining ev-ermore.

A Feast of Love To-Day.

FANNY J. CROSBY.   JNO. R. SWENEY.

DUET.

1. A feast of love to-gether, A glorious feast is ours, Where dews of
2. A feast of love to-gether, When heart and soul may rise Above these
3. A feast of love to-gether, Where God himself presides; A feast of
4. A feast of love to-gether, And while our voices blend, We look with

CHORUS.

grace are falling, Like summer's balmy show'rs.   A feast of love to-day,
earthly longings, Beyond those changing skies.
love and blessing His gracious hand provides.
ho-ly rapture To one that ne'er shall end.

To help us on our way; With Christ our elder brother, A precious feast to-day.

Copyright, 1893, by Jno. R. Sweney.

Have ye Received the Holy Ghost?

Mrs. C. H. M. Acts xix: 2. Mrs. C. H. Morris.

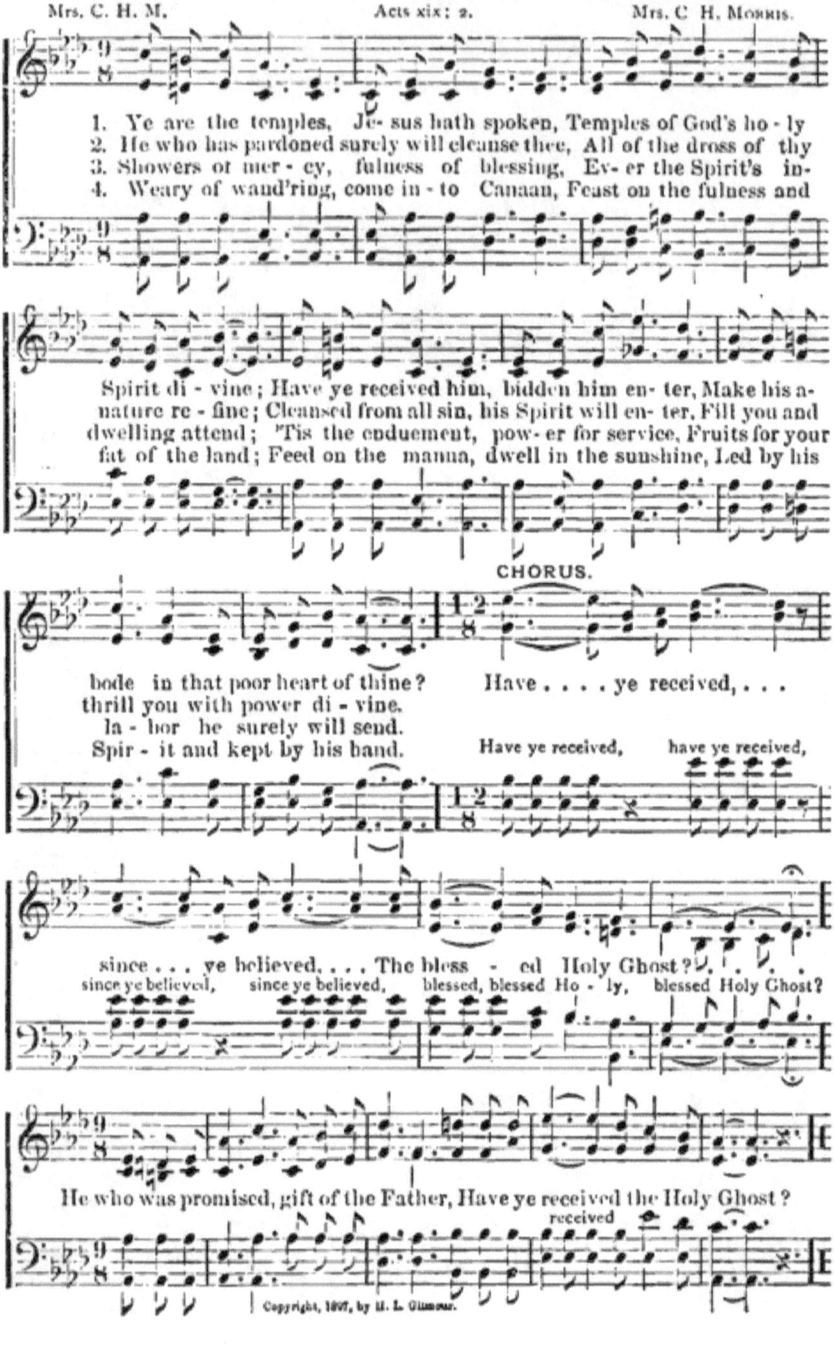

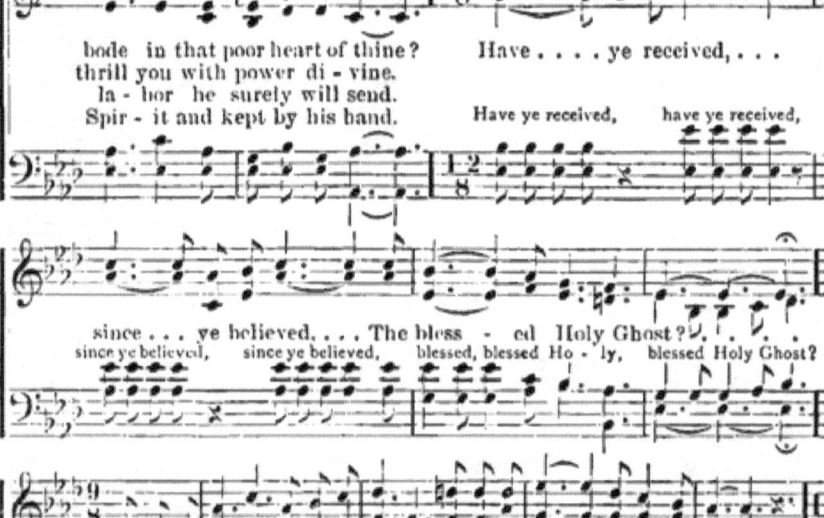

The Lord Knoweth Our Frame.

Rev. Johnson Oatman, Jr. Psalm ciii: 14. J. Howard Entwisle.

1. Christ lived and suffered here below,—The Lord knoweth our frame;
2. In him alone we put our trust,—The Lord knoweth our frame;
3. The world is not to judge us here,—The Lord knoweth our frame;

He died because he loved us so, O glory to his name!
For "he rememb'reth we are dust," O glory to his name!
We shall before his face appear, O glory to his name!

CHORUS.

The Lord knoweth our frame, . . . The Lord knoweth our frame; . . .
he knoweth our frame,   he knoweth our frame;

He remembereth we are dust, O glory to his name! . . .
ho-ly name!

4 We have an advocate with Him,—
   The Lord knoweth our frame;
   He will forgive us ev'ry sin,
   O glory to his name!

5 He will not leave us here alone,—
   The Lord knoweth our frame;
   But soon will come to call us home,
   O glory to his name!

The Harbor-Home.

Harriet E. Jones. J. Howard Entwisle.

1. You're sailing t'ward the fearful rapids, brother, Face the harbor-home! You're drifting farther from the beacon, brother, Face the harbor-home! See the clouds of darkness o'er you, See the many wrecks before you, Turn this moment, we implore you, Face the harbor-home!

2. Beware of hidden rock and sand, my brother, Face the harbor-home! Oh, turn toward the shining beacon, brother, Face the harbor-home! Shining stars their watch are keeping, Angry waves are 'round you sweeping, Guardian angels must be weeping, Face the harbor-home!

3. Before you there is awful danger, brother, Face the harbor-home! Just turn about and there is safety, brother, Face the harbor-home! Brightly now the light is burning, Wise are they the light discerning, Oh! at once your back be turning, Face the harbor-home!

CHORUS.

Face the harbor-home! Face the harbor-home! Face the harbor-home! The light discern, your frail bark turn, And face the harbor-home!

Face, O face the harbor-home! Face, O face the harbor-home! Face, O face the harbor-home! quickly face harbor-home! face the har-bor-home!

Copyright, 1897, by John J. Hood.

Great Deliverer. 157

F. M. D.
Frank M. Davis.

1. I have found a precious friend whose name is Jesus, I will praise him ever with my heart and voice; He has compass'd me with songs of sweet deliv'rance, He has made my soul with righteousness rejoice.
2. For his name's sake he forgiveth my transgressions, My in-iq-ui-ty and sin he covers o'er, And he hides me in the se-cret of his presence, He preserves me from all evil evermore.
3. This I know, he is my light and my sal-va-tion, He's an ev-er present help when trouble's nigh, In his blessed guidance I am ful-ly trusting, For he tells me "I will guide thee with mine eye."

CHORUS.

Mighty Saviour, great Deliv'rer, Who among the mighty shall be liken'd unto him? Mighty Saviour, great Deliv'rer, Who among the mighty shall be liken'd un-to him?

Copyright, 1895, by Frank M. Davis. John J. Hood, owner.

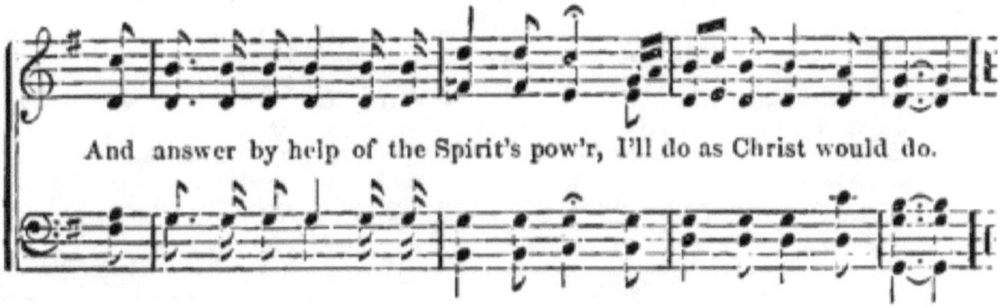

What would Jesus Do?—CONCLUDED. 159

And answer by help of the Spirit's pow'r, I'll do as Christ would do.

Just for To-day.

E. R. WILBERFORCE. H. R. PALMER.

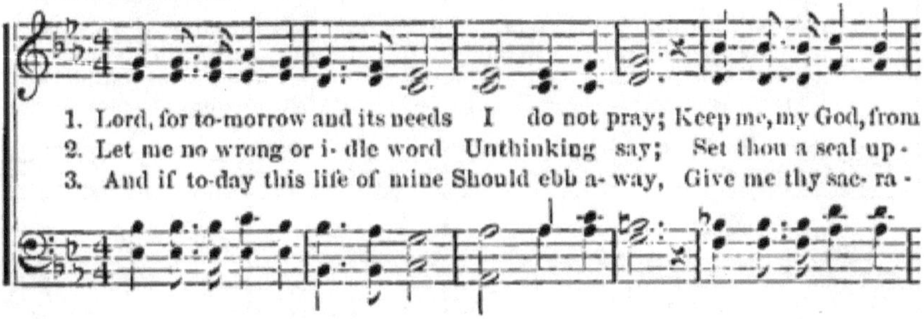

1. Lord, for to-morrow and its needs I do not pray; Keep me, my God, from
2. Let me no wrong or i-dle word Unthinking say; Set thou a seal up-
3. And if to-day this life of mine Should ebb a-way, Give me thy sacra-

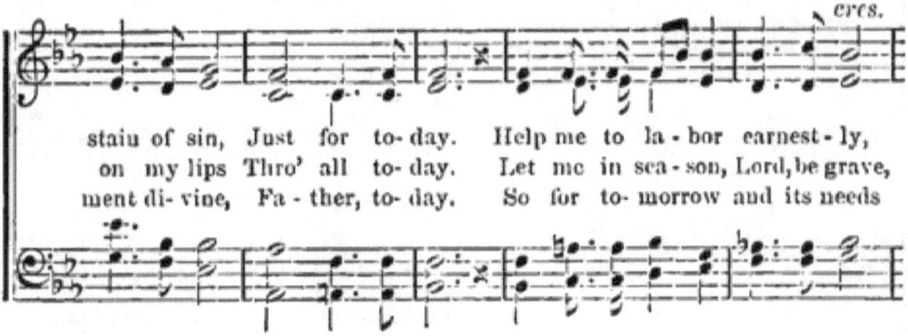

stain of sin, Just for to-day. Help me to la-bor earnest-ly,
on my lips Thro' all to-day. Let me in sea-son, Lord, be grave,
ment di-vine, Fa-ther, to-day. So for to-morrow and its needs

And du-ly pray; Let me be kind in word and deed, Father, to-day.
In season gay; Let me be faithful to thy grace, Dear Lord, to-day.
I do not pray; Still keep me, guide me, love me, Lord, Thro' each to-day.

Copyright, 1887, by H. R. Palmer. Used by per.

Glorious Victory.

161

Fanny J. Crosby.　　　　　　　　　　　　　　　　Jno. R. Sweney.

1. Vic-tory, vic-tory, glorious vic-tory, Onward, soldiers of the Lord;
2. Vic-tory, vic-tory, glorious vic-tory, Faint not, fear not, boldly stand;
3. Vic-tory, vic-tory, glorious vic-tory Still is sounding from the sky,
4. Vic-tory, vic-tory, glorious vic-tory, Soon we'll lay our armor down;

Hear the soul-in-spiring promise, We shall conquer thro' his word.
Wave our ban-ner, shout ho-san-na, With the Spirit's sword in hand.
While be-fore our great Commander Sa-tan's vanquish'd armies fly.
Soon give up the cross for-ev-er, And re-ceive the victor's crown.

CHORUS.

We shall o-ver-come the world, hal-le-lu-jah to his name,

We shall o-ver-come by faith; We shall o-ver-come the world,

hal-le-lu-jah to his name, Who has triumphed o-ver death.

Copyright, 1890, by Jno. R. Sweney.　　　　　*Love and Praise, No. 5.*—L

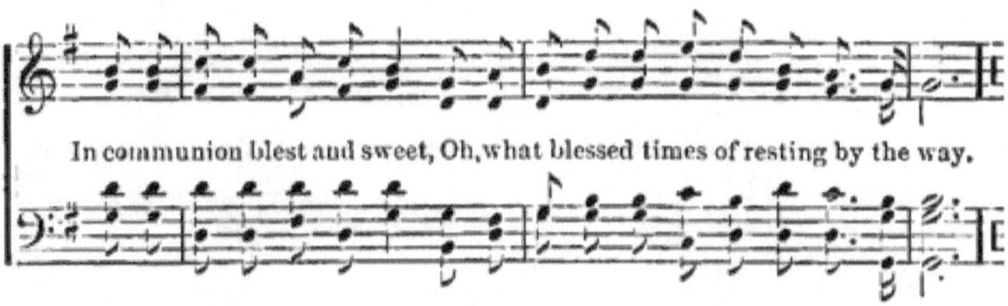

Resting By the Way.—CONCLUDED.

In communion blest and sweet, Oh, what blessed times of resting by the way.

Sunshine has Come to Me.

M. LOUISE SMITH.　　　　　　　　　　　　　HOWARD E. SMITH.

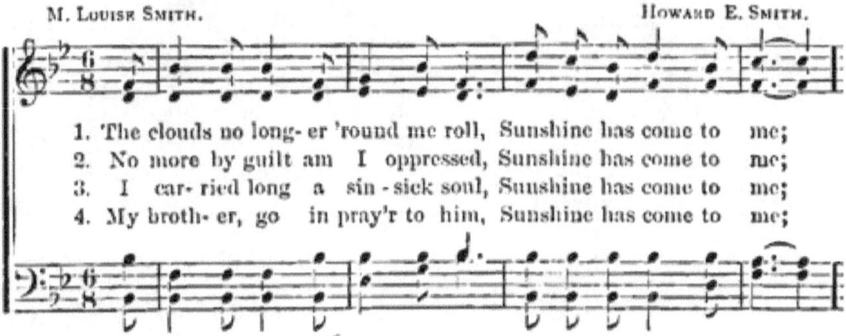

1. The clouds no long-er 'round me roll, Sunshine has come to me;
2. No more by guilt am I oppressed, Sunshine has come to me;
3. I car-ried long a sin-sick soul, Sunshine has come to me;
4. My broth-er, go in pray'r to him, Sunshine has come to me;

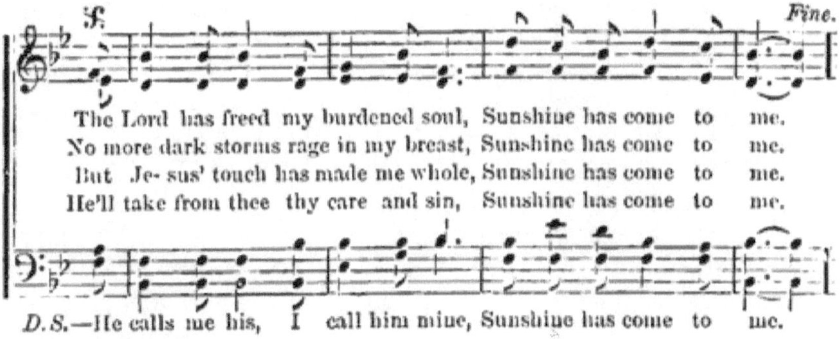

Fine.

The Lord has freed my burdened soul, Sunshine has come to me.
No more dark storms rage in my breast, Sunshine has come to me.
But Je-sus' touch has made me whole, Sunshine has come to me.
He'll take from thee thy care and sin, Sunshine has come to me.

D.S.—He calls me his, I call him mine, Sunshine has come to me.

CHORUS.　　　　　　　　　　　　　　　　　　　　　　D.S.

What bliss-ful joy! what peace divine! His pardoned child to be;

Copyright, 1890, by John J. Hood.

Why Don't You Tell It?

169

Rev. Johnson Oatman, Jr.
Jno. R. Sweney.

1. O brother, if the Lord has forgiv'n your sin, Why don't you tell it ev'rywhere you go? If thro' the door of mercy you have enter'd in, Why don't you tell it ev'rywhere you go?
2. O brother, are you leaning on the Saviour's breast? Why don't you tell it ev'rywhere you go? If you have found a haven where your soul can rest, Why don't you tell it ev'rywhere you go?
3. O brother, are you trusting in a Saviour's love? Why don't you tell it ev'rywhere you go? If you are pressing onward to that home above, Why don't you tell it ev'rywhere you go?
4. O brother, tell the story, day will soon be done, Why don't you tell it ev'rywhere you go? If you expect a mansion when your race is run, Why don't you tell it ev'rywhere you go?

CHORUS.

O brother, time is flying, O brother, men are dying, Christ died to save their souls from sin and woe; If you have been forgiven, and on your way to heaven, Why don't you tell it ev'rywhere you go?

Copyright, 1890, by Jno. R. Sweney.

My Saviour First of All.

171

FANNY J. CROSBY.
JNO. R. SWENEY.

1. When my life-work is end-ed, and I cross the swelling tide, When the bright and glorious morning I shall see; I shall know my Redeemer when I reach the oth-er side, And his smile will be the first to welcome me.
2. Oh, the soul-thrilling rapture when I view his blessed face, And the lustre of his kindly beaming eye; How my full heart will praise him for the mercy, love, and grace, That prepares for me a mansion in the sky.
3. Oh, the dear ones in glo-ry, how they beckon me to come, And our parting at the riv-er I re-call; To the sweet vales of Eden they will sing my welcome home; But I long to meet my Saviour first of all.
4. Thro' the gates to the cit-y in a robe of spotless white, He will lead me where no tears will ever fall; In the glad song of a-ges I shall mingle with delight; But I long to meet my Saviour first of all.

CHORUS.

I shall know him, I shall know him, And redeem'd by his side I shall stand,
I shall know him, I shall know him, I shall know him By the print of the nails in his hand.

Copyright, 1891, by Jno. R. Sweney.

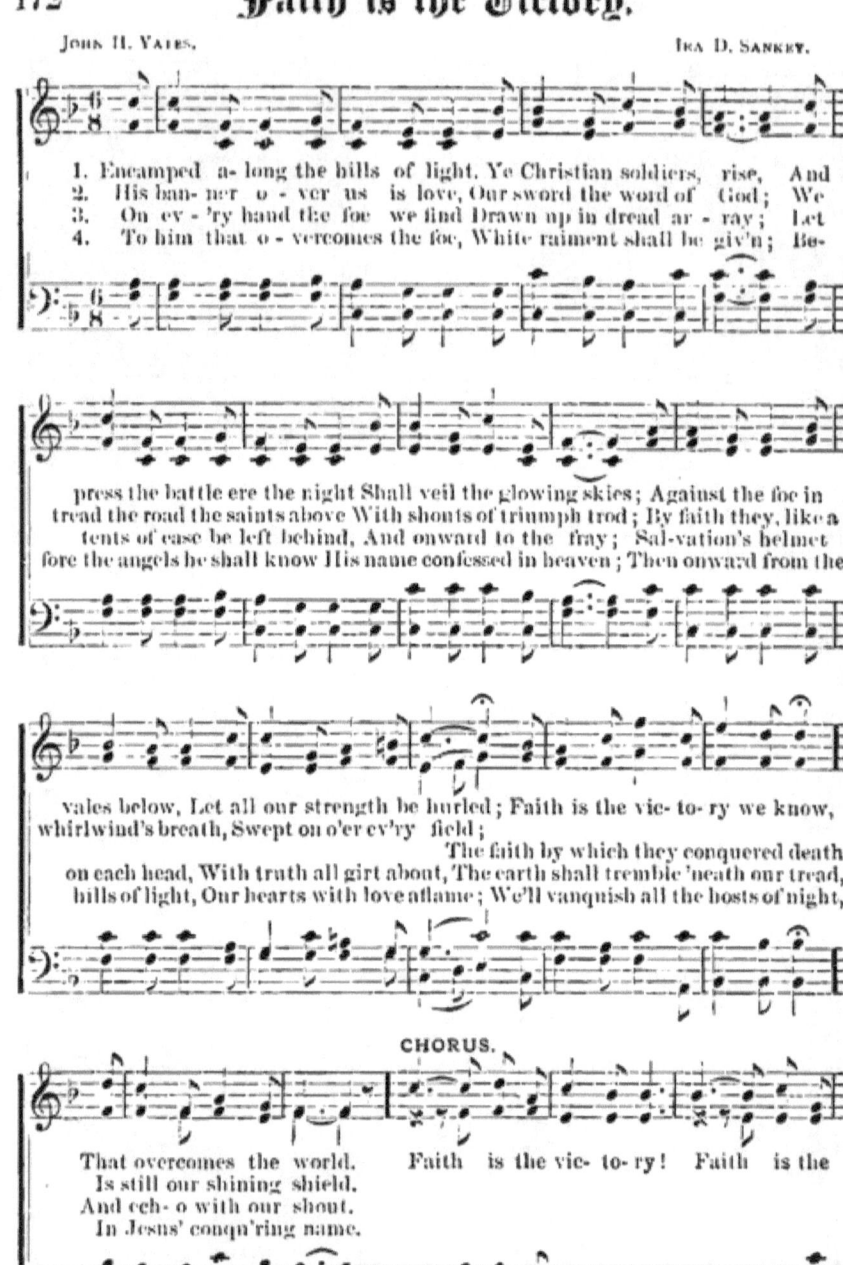

Faith is the Victory.—CONCLUDED.

In that City.

C. J. B. — CHAS. J. BUTLER.

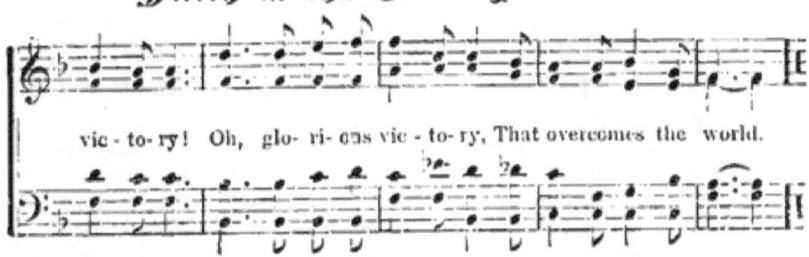

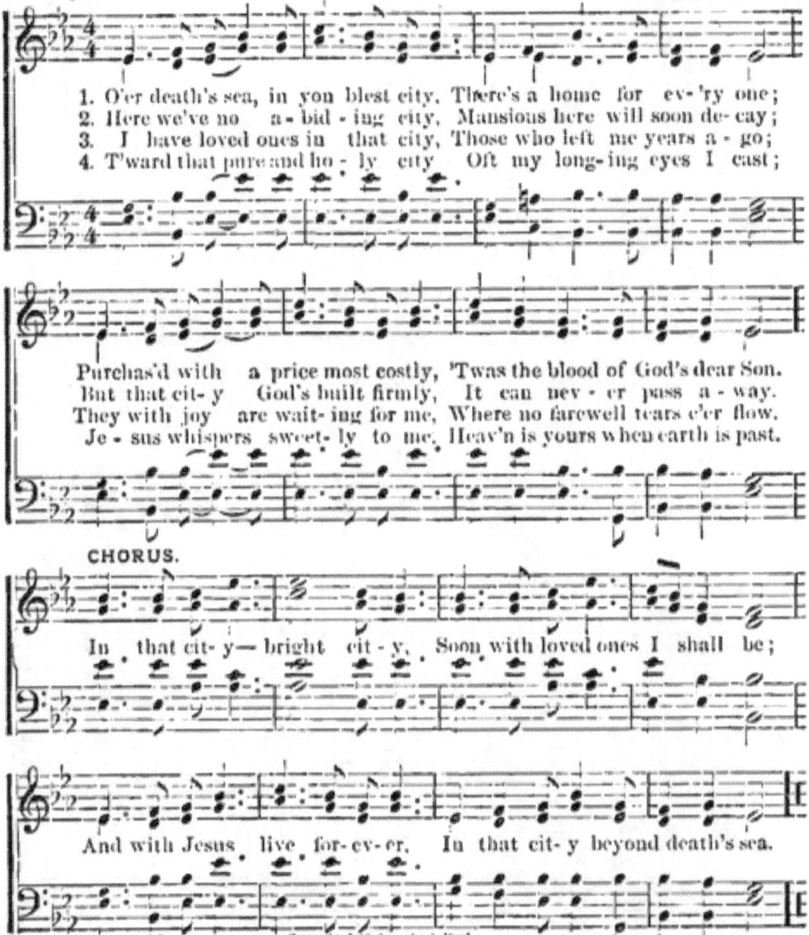

176. Sweetly I'm Resting in Jesus.

W. J. K.
WM. J. KIRKPATRICK.

1. Sweetly I'm resting in Je-sus, Trusting my Saviour and Lord;
2. Sweetly I'm resting in Je-sus, Plung'd in the life-giv-ing flood,
3. Sweetly I'm resting in Je-sus; Glo-ry-light beams on my way,
4. Sweetly I'm resting in Je-sus, Safe on his bos-om re-clined;

Casting my soul on his mer-cy, Leaning up-on his word;
Bath'd in the sea of re-demption, Wash'd in the cleansing blood;
Bright'ning my path thro' the darkness, Chasing the clouds a-way,
Tokens of per-fect sal-va-tion, Fullness of joy I find,

Bearing the cross thro' toil and pain, Counting as loss all earth-ly gain;
Passive-ly ly-ing at his feet, Learning the bliss of love complete;
Feeding in pastures green and fair, Drinking from fountains flowing there,
Pur-er and clear-er all the way, Shineth the light of per-fect day,

Knowing the faithful a crown shall obtain, Sweetly I'm resting in Je-sus.
Waiting his pleasure whatev-er is meet, Sweetly I'm resting in Je-sus.
Tender-ly guarded by his loving care Sweetly I'm resting in Je-sus.
Ho-ly the rapture, triumphant the lay, Sweetly I'm resting in Je-sus.

From "Leaflet Gems." By per. of John J. Hood.

D. S.—Blessed assurance, his name be ador'd, Sweetly I'm resting in Je-sus.

Let the Saviour In.—CONCLUDED. 179

sin; O then let the blessed Stranger in.

heart from all its sin; O then let the blessed Stranger in.

Open All the Day.

Rev. Johnson Oatman, Jr.   Rev. xxi: 25.   J. Howard Entwisle.

1. The pearl-y gates of glo-ry Are swinging wide alway, For God's own
2. They're o-pen wide for-ev-er, O brother, look that way; Behold those
3. No night there throws its shadow, They're open wide to stay, For God's own
4. So all the world may en-ter, Thro' Christ the Living Way, For since he

CHORUS.

Bi-ble tells us They're open all the day. They're open all the day, They're
gates of glo-ry, They're open all the day.
word informs us They're open all the day.
died for sinners They're open all the day.

open wide alway, Those pearly gates of glory, Oh, they're open all the day.

Copyright, 1898, by John J. Hood.

When we Reach our Home.

HARRIET E. JONES.   J. HOWARD ENTWISLE.

1. Not a cloud to hide our sky When we reach our home; Nev-er tempest sweeping by When we reach our home; Not a wave our bark to toss, Not a thought of pain or loss, Crowns of glory af-ter cross When we reach our home.
2. Never wrong against the right When we reach our home; Nev-er sin-ful hosts to fight When we reach our home; With our shining shield and sword Let us battle for our Lord, Thinking of the blest reward When we reach our home.
3. Nevermore a grave appears When we reach our home; Wip'd away are sorrow's tears When we reach our home; Not a moan above our dead, Not a lonely path to tread, Not a bitter tear to shed When we reach our home.
4. We will labor, watch and pray Till we reach our home; Cling to Christ our hope and stay Till we reach our home; All our sorrows meekly bear, Each with each life's burdens share, Thinking of the glory there When we reach our home.

CHORUS.

When we reach our home, Restful, hap - py home,
When we reach our home, sweet home,   Restful, happy home, sweet home,
Over there where the many mansions be. Bright, e-ter-nal home,
ma- ny mansions be, Bright, eternal, happy home, sweet home.

Copyright, 1897, by John J. Hood.

I was Down at the Pool.—CONCLUDED.

And found pardon in the waters, When the Spirit came in mighty pow'r.

mighty pow'r.

Where He Leadeth.

"He goeth before them, and the sheep follow him."—John x: 4.

FANNY J. CROSBY.   FRANK M. DAVIS.

1. Where my Shepherd leads I'll fol-low, Follow in his own right way;
2. Where my Shepherd leads I'll fol-low, Tho' the way be dark and drear;
3. Where my Shepherd leads I'll fol-low, Fully trusting as I go;

If his hand is always guid-ing, I can nev-er go a-stray.
If my Saviour's hand is lead-ing, I shall nev-er, nev-er fear.
Thro' green pastures he will lead me, Where the living wa-ters flow.

CHORUS.

Where he leadeth I will fol-low, Follow Je-sus all the way;
follow, follow,

Where he leadeth I will fol-low, Follow Je-sus all the way.
follow, follow,

From "Brightest Glory." By per. of John J. Hood.

Redeemed thro' the Blood.—CONCLUDED. 195

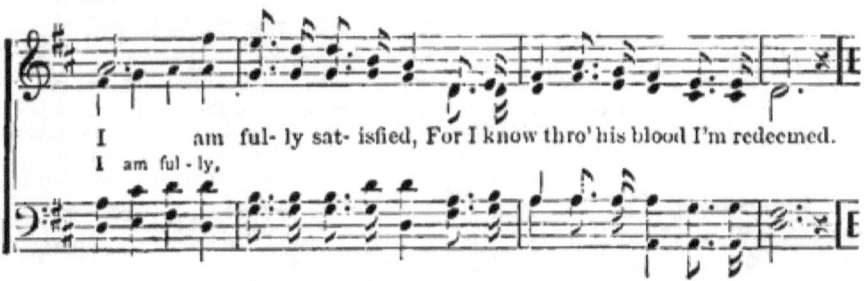

On the Way.

LIZZIE EDWARDS. JNO. R. SWENEY.

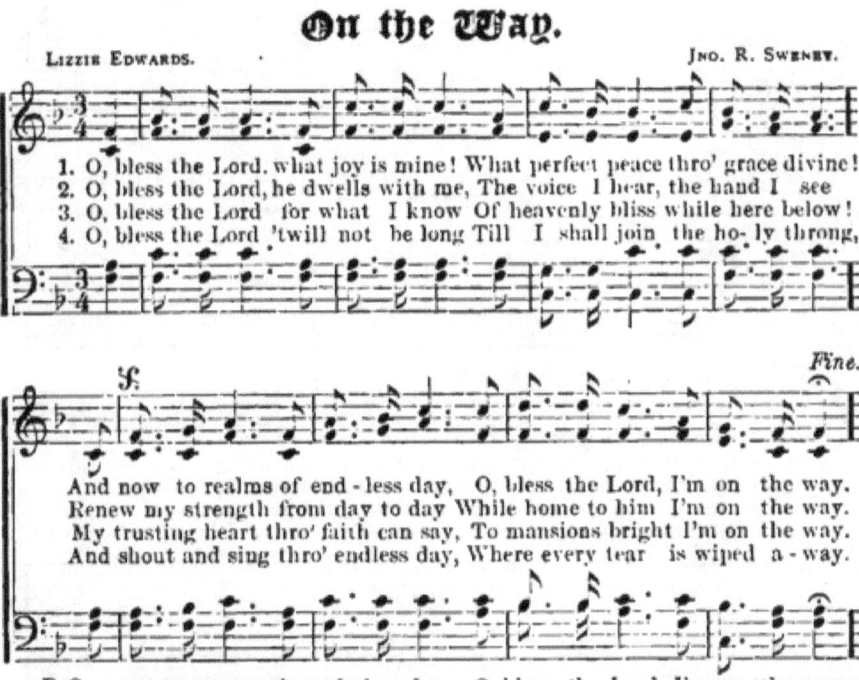

Copyright, 1890, by Jno. R. Sweney.

The Best Friend is Jesus.—CONCLUDED. 197

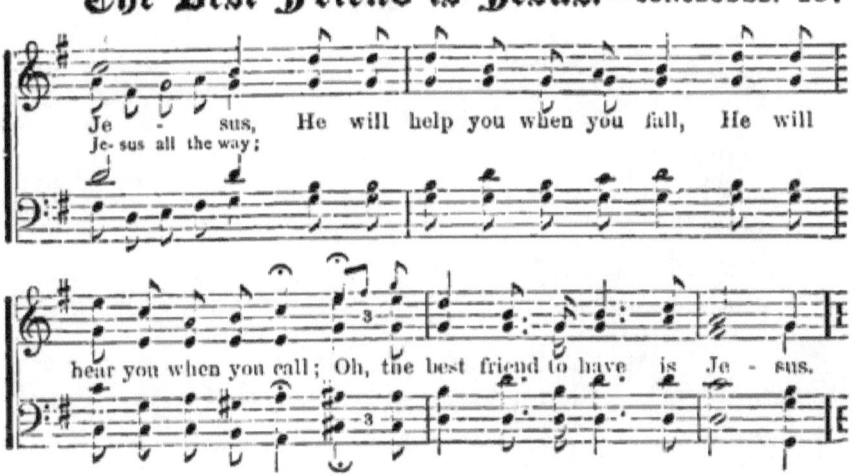

The Golden Key.

"Prayer is the key to unlock the door, and the bolt to shut in the night"

JNO. R. SWENEY.

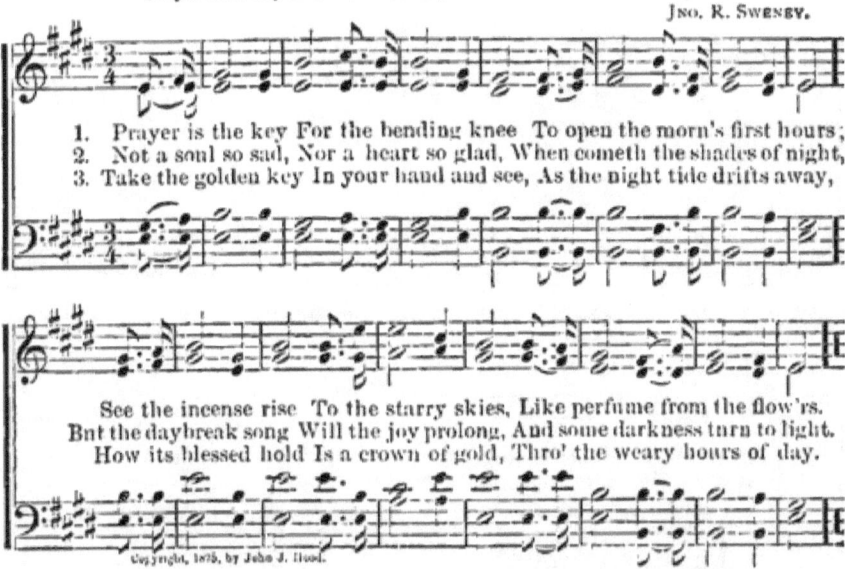

1. Prayer is the key For the bending knee To open the morn's first hours;
2. Not a soul so sad, Nor a heart so glad, When cometh the shades of night,
3. Take the golden key In your hand and see, As the night tide drifts away,

See the incense rise To the starry skies, Like perfume from the flow'rs.
But the daybreak song Will the joy prolong, And some darkness turn to light.
How its blessed hold Is a crown of gold, Thro' the weary hours of day.

Copyright, 1875, by John J. Hood.

4 When the shadows fall,
  And the vesper call
Is sobbing its low refrain,
  'Tis a garland sweet
  To the toil-dent feet,
And an antidote for pain.

5 Soon the year's dark door
  Shall be shut no more:
Life's tears shall be wiped away,
  As the pearl gates swing,
  And the gold harps ring,
And the sun unsheathes for aye.

198. I Love Him Far Better.

E. G. C.
Eli G. Christy.

1. It pays to serve Jesus, I speak from my heart; He'll always be with us, if we do our part; There's naught in this wide world can pleasure afford, There's peace and contentment in serving the Lord.
2. And oft when I'm tempted to turn from the track, I think of my Saviour,—my mind wanders back To the place where they nailed him on Calvary's tree—I hear a voice saying,—I suffered for thee!
3. There's a place that remembrance still brings back to me, 'Twas there I found pardon,—'twas heaven to me; There Jesus spoke sweetly to my weary soul, My sins are forgiven, he made my heart whole.
4. How rich is the blessing the world cannot give, I'm satisfied fully for Jesus to live, Tho' friends may forsake me and trials arise, I am trusting in Jesus—his love never dies.

D. S.—ever the cost, I'll be a true soldier,—I'll die at my post.

CHORUS.

{ I love him far better than in days of yore, }
{ I'll serve him more truly than ever before, } I'll do as he bids me what-

Copyright, 1894, by Jno. R. Sweney.

5 Will you have this blessing that Jesus bestows,
A free, full salvation—as ev'ry one knows?
Oh, sinner, poor sinner, to Calvary flee,
The blood of my Saviour was shed there for thee.

6 There is no one like Jesus, can cheer me to-day, [away,
His love and his kindness can ne'er fade
In winter, in summer, in sunshine and rain, [same.
His love and affection are always the

Jesus Leads.

199

"And when he putteth forth his own sheep, he goeth before them, and the sheep follow him; for they know his voice."—John x: 4.

JOHN R. CLEMENTS.   JNO. R. SWENEY.

Andante.

1. Like a shepherd, tender, true, Jesus leads, . . . Jesus leads, . .
2. All a-long life's rugged road Jesus leads, . . . Jesus leads, . .
3. Thro' the sun-lit ways of life Jesus leads, . . . Jesus leads, . .

Daily finds us pastures new, Jesus leads, . . . Jesus leads; . .
Till we reach yon blest a-bode, Jesus leads, . . . Jesus leads; . .
Thro' the war-ings and the strife Jesus leads, . . . Jesus leads; . .

If thick mists are o'er the way, . . Or the flock 'mid danger feeds, . .
All the way, . before, he's trod, . And he now . . the flock precedes, . .
When we reach . the Jordan's tide, Where life's bound-'ry-line re-cedes, . .

rit.

He will watch them lest they stray, Jesus leads, . . Jesus leads.
Safe in-to the fold of God Jesus leads, . . Jesus leads.
He will spread the waves a-side, Jesus leads, . . Jesus leads.

Copyright, 1890, by Jno. R. Sweney.

I will Say "Yes" to Jesus.—CONCLUDED. 201

With outstretch'd hands my Saviour stands, And beckons the wand'rer to come; the wand'rer to come;

Without de- lay I'll now o- bey, And he will welcome me home. ... will welcome me home.

Whosoever Believeth.

Rev. FREDERICK DENISON. W. WARREN BENTLEY. By per.

1. From Calv'ry's mountain sounding, What loving words we hear, The love of
2. Oh, seek this great sal- vation, And cast out ev-'ry sin, The soul's e-
3. Who- e'er my Word be- lieveth, We hear the Saviour say, A par- don
4. O brother, come and trust him, O come to him to - day, He's waiting

CHORUS.

God a- bounding, Dispell- ing all our fear. O brother, believe it!
man- ci - pa- tion, By pow'r divine with- in.
full re - ceiveth, All sins are wash'd away.
to re- ceive you, Why longer, then, delay?

O brother, receive it! Whoso- ev- er believeth Hath everlast - ing life.

205. Once Upon a Stormy Ocean.

Arranged and harmonized by J. H. E.

1. Once upon a stormy ocean Rode a bark at eventide,
While the waves in wild commotion Dashed against the vessel's side;

D.S.—While the winds were all abroad Calmly slept the Son of God.

Jesus sleeping on a pillow Heeded not the raging billow,

2 In that dark and stormy hour
   Fearful ones awoke their Lord,
Jesus by his sovereign power
   Calmed the tempest with a word;
Out on life's tempestuous ocean,
   'Mid the billows' wild commotion,
Trembling soul, your Lord is there,
   He will make you still his care.

3 Jesus knows your silent weeping
   When before his cross you bow,
Never, never is he sleeping,
   Where he reigns in glory now;
If the world be dark before thee,
   And the billows rolling o'er thee,
Should thy soul with terror fill,
   Hear Christ saying, "peace, be still."

206. The Old Folks' Hymn.

I was in the home of an aged couple one day; their little granddaughter went singing through the house, "What a friend we have in Jesus." The tears coursed down their wrinkled faces and they said, "these words we realize to be true in our case."—C. J. B.
C. J. B.

CHAS. J. BUTLER.

1. I sat within a home one day With two whose locks with age were gray,
2. The tears cours'd down their aged face, Where grief's rude hand had left its trace,
3. Those aged ones long years ago In triumph left this world of woe;

Copyright, 1877, by John J. Hood.

The Old Folks' Hymn.—CONCLUDED.

The heav'nly race they long had run, Their work on earth was nearly done;
And 'mid those tears to me they said, "On Christ long since our care we've laid,
They're living now with Christ their friend, And joys are their's which ne'er shall end.

Within that humble home was one Who had life's journey just begun,
He's been to us a friend so dear, In sorrow's night spoke words of cheer,"
The song of that far, dis-tant day From mem'ry ne'er will fade a-way;

And with her childish voice sang clear This dear old hymn, so full of cheer.*
They prais'd the One once for them slain, While still she sang this sweet refrain.†
When burden'd with earth's care and grief I've sung this song and found relief.‡

207 What a Friend We Have in Jesus.
(May be sung by a little girl.)

1. What a Friend we have in, etc.

*1 What a Friend we have in Jesus,
   All our sins and griefs to bear!
 What a privilege to carry
   Everything to God in prayer!
 O what peace we often forfeit,
   O what needless pain we bear
 All because we do not carry
   Everything to God in prayer!

†2 Have we trials and temptations?
   Is there trouble anywhere?
 We should never be discouraged,
   Take it to the Lord in prayer.
 Can we find a friend so faithful
   Who will all our sorrows share?
 Jesus knows our every weakness,
   Take it to the Lord in prayer.

‡3 Are we weak and heavy laden,
   Cumbered with a load of care?
 Precious Saviour, still our refuge,—
   Take it to the Lord in prayer.
 Do thy friends despise, forsake thee?
   Take it to the Lord in prayer;
 In his arms he'll take and shield thee,
   Thou wilt find a solace there

208. Nearer, My God, to Thee!

Mrs. Sarah F. Adams.   Rev. S. G. Neil.

1. Nearer, my God, to thee! Nearer to thee,
E'en tho' it be a cross (*Omit*......) That raiseth me;
Still all my song shall be, Nearer, my God, to thee,
Nearer, my God, to thee! (*Omit*......) Nearer to thee!

2 Though like the wanderer,
The sun gone down,
Darkness be over me,
My rest a stone,
Yet in my dreams I'd be
Nearer, my God, to thee,
Nearer to thee!

3 There let the way appear,
Steps unto heaven;
All that thou sendest me,
In mercy given,
Angels to beckon me
Nearer, my God, to thee,
Nearer to thee!

4 Then, with my waking thoughts
Bright with thy praise,
Out of my stony griefs
Bethel I'll raise;
So by my woes to be
Nearer, my God, to thee,
Nearer to thee!

5 Or if, on joyful wing
Cleaving the sky,
Sun, moon, and stars forgot,
Upward I fly,
Still all my song shall be,
Nearer, my God, to thee,
Nearer to thee!

---

209. My Country! 'Tis of Thee.

My country! 'tis of thee,
Sweet land of liberty,
  Of thee I sing:
Land where my fathers died!
Land of the pilgrim's pride!
From every mountain side
  Let freedom ring!

2 My native country, thee,
Land of the noble, free,
  Thy name I love;
I love thy rocks and rills,
Thy woods and templed hills:
My heart with rapture thrills
  Like that above.

3 Let music swell the breeze,
And ring from all the trees
  Sweet freedom's song:
Let mortal tongues awake;
Let all that breathe partake;
Let rocks their silence break,
  The sound prolong.

4 Our father's God! to thee,
Author of liberty,
  To thee we sing:
Long may our land be bright
With freedom's holy light;
Protect us by thy might,
  Great God, our King!

210. Jesus, the Name.

C. WESLEY. Tune, CORONATION. C. M.

1. Je-sus! the name high o-ver all, In hell, or earth, or sky;
   An-gels and men be-fore it fall, And dev-ils fear and fly.

2. Je-sus! the name to sin-ners dear, The name to sin-ners given;
   It scat-ters all their guilt-y fear; It turns their hell to heaven.

3 Jesus the prisoner's fetters breaks,
  And bruises Satan's head ;
  Power into strengthless souls he speaks,
  And life into the dead.

4 O that the world might taste and see
  The riches of his grace !
  The arms of love that compass me
  Would all mankind embrace.

5 His only righteousness I show
  His saving truth proclaim :
  'Tis all my business here below,
  To cry, " Behold the Lamb!"

6 Happy, if with my latest breath
  I may but gasp his name;
  Preach him to all, and cry in death,
  " Behold, behold the Lamb!"

211. Crown Him Lord of All.
C. M.

1 All hail the power of Jesus' name !
  Let angels prostrate fall;
  Bring forth the royal diadem,
  And crown him Lord of all.

2 Crown him, ye morning stars of light,
  Who fixed this earthly ball;
  Now hail the strength of Israel's might,
  And crown him Lord of all.

3 Ye chosen seed of Israel's race,
  Ye ransomed from the fall,
  Hail him who saves you by his grace,
  And crown him Lord of all.

4 Sinners, whose love can ne'er forget
  The wormwood and the gall,
  Go, spread your trophies at his feet,
  And crown him Lord of all.

5 Let every kindred, every tribe,
  On this terrestrial ball,
  To him all majesty ascribe
  And crown him Lord of all.

6 O that with yonder sacred throng
  We at his feet may fall !
  We'll join the everlasting song,
  And crown him Lord of all.

Hamburg. L. M.

212 While Life Prolongs.

1 While life prolongs its precious light
  Mercy is found, and peace is given,
But soon, ah! soon, approaching night
  Shall blot out every hope of heaven.

2 While God invites, how blest the day,
  How sweet the Gospel's charming sound;
Come, sinners, haste, oh, haste away,
  While yet a pardoning God is found.

3 Soon, borne on time's most rapid wing,
  Shall death command you to the grave;
Before his bar your spirits bring,
  And none be found to hear or save.

4 In that lone land of deep despair,
  No Sabbath's heavenly light shall rise—
No God regard your bitter prayer,
  No Saviour call you to the skies.

213 Just as I am.

1 Just as I am, without one plea,
But that thy blood was shed for me,
And that thou bids't me come to thee,
O Lamb of God, I come! I come!

2 Just as I am, and waiting not
To rid my soul of one dark blot, [spot,
To thee, whose blood can cleanse each
O Lamb of God, I come! I come!

3 Just as I am, though tossed about
With many a conflict, many a doubt,
Fightings within and fears without,
O Lamb of God, I come! I come!

4 Just as I am—poor, wretched, blind;
Sight, riches, healing of the mind,
Yea, all I need, in thee to find,
O Lamb of God, I come! I come!

5 Just as I am—thou wilt receive,
Wilt welcome, pardon, cleanse, relieve,
Because thy promise I believe,
O Lamb of God, I come! I come!

6 Just as I am—thy love unknown
Hath broken every barrier down;
Now, to be thine, yea, thine alone,
O Lamb of God, I come! I come!

214 Come, Holy Spirit.

1 Come, Holy Spirit, calm my mind,
  And fit me to approach my God;
Remove each vain, each worldly thought,
  And lead me to thy blest abode.

2 Hast thou imparted to my soul
  A living spark of holy fire?
Oh! kindle now the sacred flame,
  Make me to burn with pure desire.

3 A brighter faith and hope impart,
  And let me now my Saviour see;
Oh! soothe and cheer my burdened heart,
  And bid my spirit rest in thee.

215 When I Survey.

1 When I survey the wondrous cross,
  On which the Prince of Glory died,
My richest gain I count but loss,
  And pour contempt on all my pride.

2 Forbid it, Lord, that I should boast,
  Save in the death of Christ, my God;
All the vain things that charm me most,
  I sacrifice them to his blood.

3 See, from his head, his hands, his feet,
  Sorrow and love flow mingled down;
Did e'er such love and sorrow meet,
  Or thorns compose so rich a crown?

4 His dying crimson, like a robe,
  Spreads o'er his body on the tree,
Then am I dead to all the globe,
  And all the globe is dead to me.

5 Were the whole realm of nature mine,
  That were a present far too small;
Love so amazing, so divine,
  Demands my soul, my life, my all.

Boylston. S. M.

LOWELL MASON.

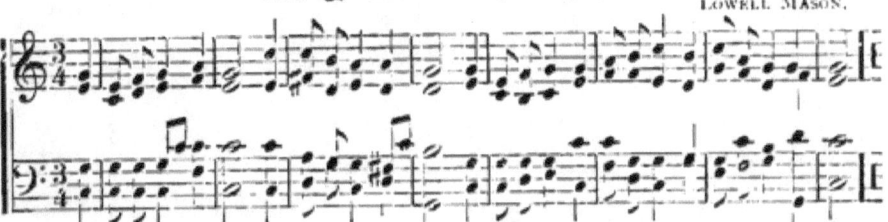

216 And can I yet Delay?

And can I yet delay
  My little all to give?
To tear my soul from earth away
  For Jesus to receive?

2 Nay, but I yield, I yield;
  I can hold out no more:
I sink, by dying love compelled,
  And own thee conqueror.

3 Though late, I all forsake;
  My friends, my all resign:
Gracious Redeemer, take, oh, take,
  And seal me ever thine.

4 Come, and possess me whole,
  Nor hence again remove;
Settle and fix my wavering soul
  With all thy weight of love.

217 A Charge to Keep I Have.

A charge to keep I have,
  A God to glorify;
A never-dying soul to save,
  And fit it for the sky.

2 To serve the present age,
  My calling to fulfill,—
Oh, may it all my powers engage
  To do my Master's will.

3 Arm me with jealous care,
  As in thy sight to live;
And oh, thy servant, Lord, prepare,
  A strict account to give.

4 Help me to watch and pray,
  And on thyself rely.
Assured, if I my trust betray,
  I shall forever die.

Laban. S. M.

218 Come, Ye that Love the Lord.

Come, ye that love the Lord,
  And let your joys be known;
Join in a song with sweet accord,
  While ye surround his throne.

2 Let those refuse to sing
  Who never knew our God,
But servants of the heavenly King
  May speak their joys abroad.

3 The men of grace have found
  Glory begun below;
Celestial fruit on earthly ground
  From faith and hope may grow:

4 Then let our songs abound,
  And every tear be dry;
We're marching through Immanuel's
  To fairer worlds on high. [ground,

219 My Soul, be on Thy Guard.

My soul, be on thy guard,
  Ten thousand foes arise,
And hosts of sin are pressing hard
  To draw thee from the skies.

2 Oh, watch, and fight, and pray,
  The battle ne'er give o'er;
Renew it boldly every day,
  And help divine implore.

3 Ne'er think the victory won,
  Nor once at ease sit down;
Thine arduous work will not be done
  Till thou hast got the crown.

4 Fight on, my soul, till death
  Shall bring thee to thy God;
He'll take thee, at thy parting breath,
  Up to his blest abode.

220 **The Morning Light.**
Samuel F. Smith. Tune, WEBB. 7, 6.

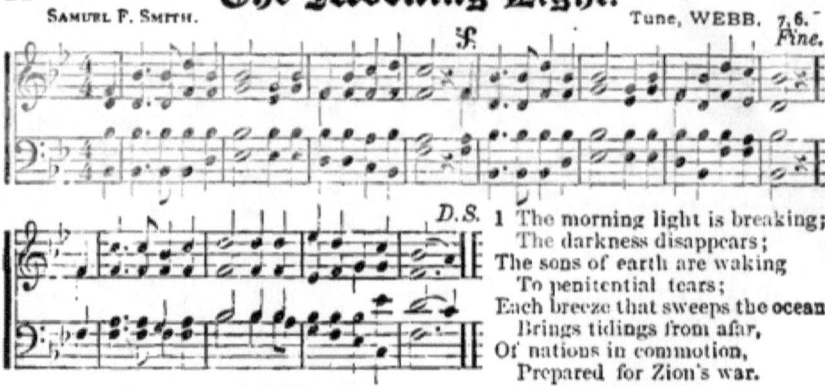

1 The morning light is breaking;
   The darkness disappears;
  The sons of earth are waking
   To penitential tears;
  Each breeze that sweeps the ocean
   Brings tidings from afar,
  Of nations in commotion,
   Prepared for Zion's war.

2 See heathen nations bending
   Before the God we love,
  And thousand hearts ascending
   In gratitude above;
  While sinners, now confessing,
   The gospel call obey,
  And seek the Saviour's blessing,
   A nation in a day.

3 Blest river of salvation,
   Pursue thine onward way;
  Flow thou to every nation,
   Nor in thy richness stay:
  Stay not till all the lowly
   Triumphant reach their home;
  Stay not till all the holy
   Proclaim, "The Lord is come!"

221 Geo. Duffield, Jr. **Stand up, stand up for Jesus.** Tune above.

1 Stand up, stand up for Jesus,
   Ye soldiers of the cross;
  Lift high his royal banner,
   It must not suffer loss;
  From victory unto victory
   His army shall he lead
  Till every foe is vanquished
   And Christ is Lord indeed.

2 Stand up, stand up for Jesus,
   The trumpet call obey;
  Forth to the mighty conflict,
   In this his glorious day:
  "Ye that are men, now serve him,"
   Against unnumbered foes:
  Your courage rise with danger,
   And strength to strength oppose.

3 Stand up, stand up for Jesus,
   Stand in his strength alone;
  The arm of flesh will fail you;
   Ye dare not trust your own:
  Put on the gospel armor,
   Each piece put on with prayer;
  Where duty calls, or danger,
   Be never wanting there.

4 Stand up, stand up for Jesus,
   The strife will not be long;
  This day the noise of battle,
   The next the victor's song:
  To him that overcometh,
   A crown of life shall be;
  He with the King of glory
   Shall reign eternally.

222 **Work, for the Night is Coming.**

1 Work, for the night is coming,
   Work through the morning hours;
  Work, while the dew is sparkling,
   Work 'mid springing flowers;
  Work, when the days grow brighter,
   Work in the glowing sun;
  Work, for the night is coming,
   When man's work is done.

2 Work, for the night is coming,
   Work through the sunny noon;
  Fill brightest hours with labor,
   Rest comes sure and soon,
  Give every flying minute
   Something to keep in store:
  Work, for the night is coming,
   When man works no more.

3 Work, for the night is coming,
   Under the sunset skies;
  While their bright tints are glowing,
   Work, for daylight flies.
  Work till the last beam fadeth,
   Fadeth to shine no more;
  Work while the night is darkening,
   When man's work is o'er.

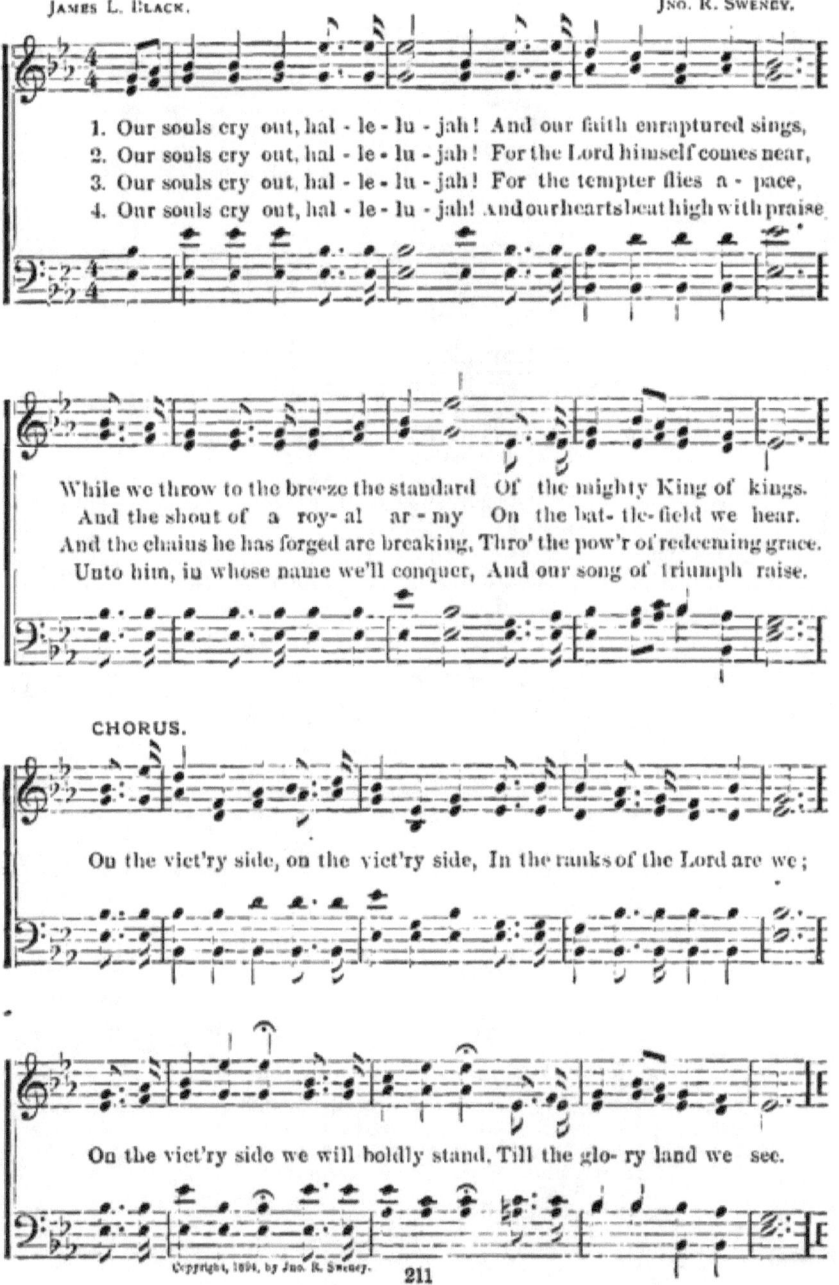

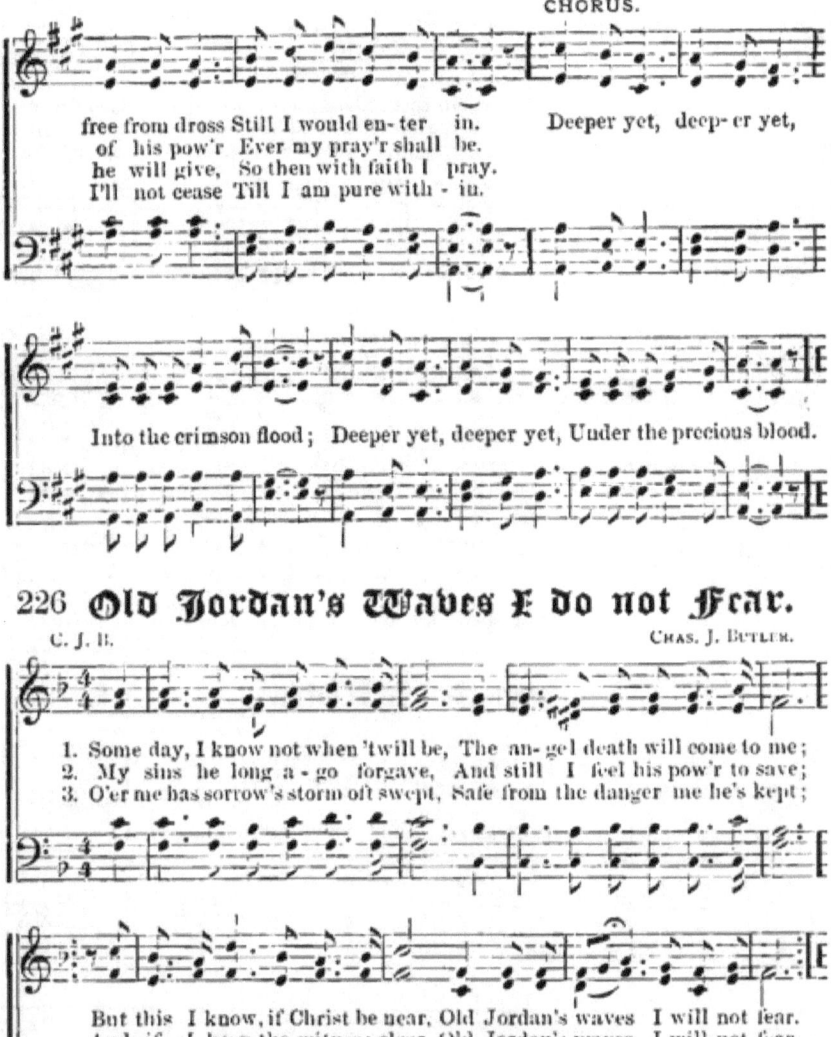

4 My lov'd ones they have cross'd the tide,
But safely cross'd with Christ their guide;
They sweetly whispered in my ear,
Old Jordan's waves I do not fear.

5 So when at death's cold brink I stand,
My hand clasp'd in the Saviour's hand;
I too shall shout in tones so clear,
Old Jordan's waves I do not fear.

227. I'll Live for Him.
C. R. Dunbar

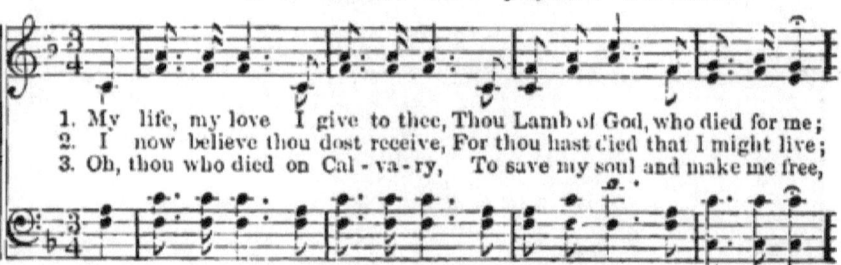

1. My life, my love I give to thee, Thou Lamb of God, who died for me;
2. I now believe thou dost receive, For thou hast died that I might live;
3. Oh, thou who died on Cal-va-ry, To save my soul and make me free,

CHO.—I'll live for him who died for me, How happy then my life shall be!

Oh, may I ev-er faith-ful be, My Sav-iour and my God!
And now henceforth I'll trust in thee, My Sav-iour and my God!
I con-se-crate my life to thee, My Sav-iour and my God!

I'll live for him who died for me, My Sav-iour and my God!

Copyright of R. E. Hudson, used by per.

228. He is Calling.
Arr. by S. J. Vail.

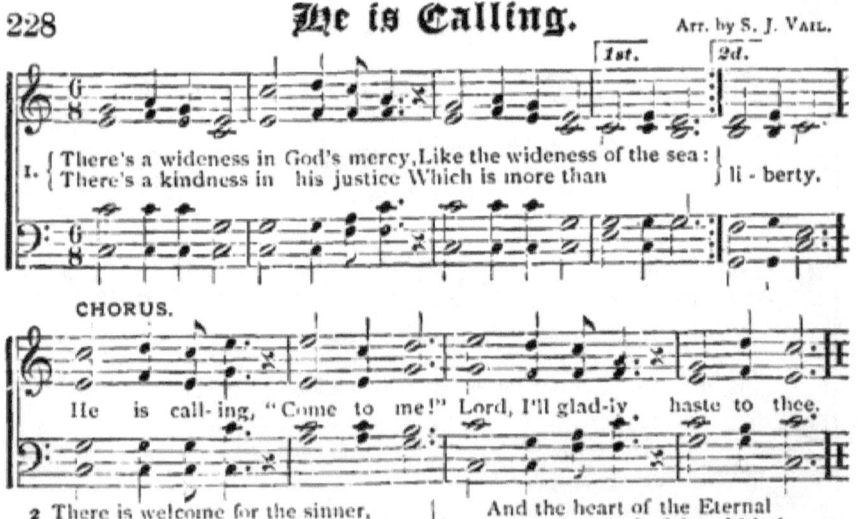

1. There's a wideness in God's mercy, Like the wideness of the sea:
There's a kindness in his justice Which is more than liberty.

CHORUS.
He is call-ing, "Come to me!" Lord, I'll glad-ly haste to thee.

2 There is welcome for the sinner,
  And more graces for the good;
There is mercy with the Saviour;
  There is healing in his blood.
3 For the love of God is broader
  Than the measure of man's mind;

And the heart of the Eternal
  Is most wonderful and kind.
4 If our love were but more simple,
  We should take him at his word;
And our lives would be all sunshine
  In the sweetness of our Lord.

229. Come, Holy Spirit. — I. Watts. — Tune, ST. MARTIN'S. C. M.

1. Come, Holy Spirit, heavenly Dove, With all thy quick'ning powers; Kindle a flame of sacred love In these cold hearts of ours.

2 Look how we grovel here below,
  Fond of these earthly toys;
  Our souls, how heavily they go,
  To reach eternal joys.

3 In vain we tune our formal songs,
  In vain we strive to rise;
  Hosannas languish on our tongues,
  And our devotion dies.

4 Father, and shall we ever live
  At this poor dying rate,
  Our love so faint, so cold to thee,
  And thine to us so great?

5 Come, Holy Spirit, heavenly Dove,
  With all thy quick'ning powers;
  Come, shed abroad a Saviour's love,
  And that shall kindle ours.

230. Come, Ye Sinners. — Joseph Hart. — Tune, GREENVILLE. 8,7,4.

1 Come, ye sinners, poor and needy,
  Weak and wounded, sick and sore;
  Jesus ready stands to save you,
    Full of pity, love, and power:
      He is able,
    He is willing: doubt no more.

2 Now, ye needy, come and welcome;
  God's free bounty glorify;
  True belief and true repentance,
    Every grace that brings you nigh,
      Without money,
    Come to Jesus Christ and buy.

3 Let not conscience make you linger,
  Nor of fitness fondly dream;
  All the fitness he requireth
    Is to feel your need of him
      This he gives you;
    'Tis the Spirit's glimmering beam.

4 Come, ye weary, heavy-laden,
  Bruised and mangled by the fall;
  If you tarry till you're better,
    You will never come at all;
      Not the righteous—
    Sinners Jesus came to call.

5 Agonizing in the garden,
  Your Redeemer prostrate lies;
  On the bloody tree behold him!
    Hear him cry, before he dies,
      "It is finished!"
    Sinners, will not this suffice?

6 Lo! the incarnate God, ascending,
  Pleads the merit of his blood;
  Venture on him, venture freely;
    Let no other trust intrude:
      None but Jesus
    Can do helpless sinners good.

FAMILIAR HYMNS.

231 Is my Name Written There. (Cop.)

Lord, I care not for riches,
  Neither silver nor gold;
I would make sure of heaven,
  I would enter the fold.
In the book of thy kingdom,
  With its pages so fair,
Tell me, Jesus, my Saviour,
  Is my name written there?

Cho.—Is my name written there,
    On the page white and fair?
  In the book of thy kingdom,
    Is my name written there?

2 Lord, my sins are so many,
    Like the sands of the sea,
  But thy blood, oh, my Saviour!
    Is sufficient for me;
  For thy promise is written,
    In bright letters that glow,
  "Though your sins be as scarlet,
    I will make them like snow."

3 Oh! that beautiful city,
    With its mansions of light,
  With its glorified beings,
    In pure garments of white;
  Where no evil thing cometh,
    To despoil what is fair;
  Where the angels are watching—
    Is my name written there?—M. A. K.

232 My Jesus, I Love Thee. (Cop.)

My Jesus, I love thee, I know thou art mine,
For thee all the follies of sin I resign;
My gracious Redeemer, my Saviour art thou,
If ever I loved thee, my Jesus, 'tis now.

2 I love thee because thou hast first loved me,
And purchased my pardon on Calvary's tree;
I love thee for wearing the thorns on thy brow;
If ever I loved thee, my Jesus, 'tis now.

3 I will love thee in life, I'll love thee in death,
And praise thee as long as thou lendest me
                                    [my brow,
    breath;
And say, when the death-dew lies cold on
If ever I loved thee, my Jesus, 'tis now.

4 In mansions of glory and endless delight
I'll ever adore thee in heaven so bright,
I'll sing with the glittering crown on my brow,
If ever I loved thee, my Jesus, 'tis now.
                           —London Hymn Book.

233 Standing on the Promises. (Cop.)

Standing on the promises of Christ my King,
Thro' eternal ages let his praises ring;
Glory in the highest I will shout and sing,
  Standing on the promises of God.

Cho.—Standing, standing,   [iour;
  Standing on the promises of God my Sav-
      Standing, standing,
  I'm standing on the promises of God.

2 Standing on the promises that cannot fail,
  When the howling storms of doubt and fear
                                    assail,
  By the living word of God I shall prevail,
    Standing on the promises of God.

3 Standing on the promises I now can see
  Perfect, present cleansing in the blood for me:
  Standing in the liberty where Christ makes
    Standing on the promises of God. [free,

4 Standing on the promises of Christ the Lord,
  Bound to him eternally by love's strong cord,
  Overcoming daily with the Spirit's sword,
    Standing on the promises of God.

5 Standing on the promises I cannot fall,
  List'ning ev'ry moment to the Spirit's call,
  Resting in my Saviour, as my all in all,
    Standing on the promises of God.
                              —R. Kelso Carter.

234 We'll Never Say Good By. (Cop.)

Our friends on earth we meet with pleas-
                                    ure,
  While swift the moments fly,
Yet ever comes the thought of sadness
  That we must say good by.

Cho.—We'll never say good by in heav'n,
    We'll never say good by,
  For in that land of joy and song,
    We'll never say good by.

2 How joyful is the thought that lingers,
    When loved ones cross death's sea,
  That when our labors here are ended,
    With them we'll ever be.

3 No parting words shall e'er be spoken
    In that bright land of flowers,
  But songs of joy, and peace, and gladness,
    Shall evermore be ours.
                        —Mrs. E. W. Chapman.

235. Fill Me Now. (Copyright.)

Hover o'er me, Holy Spirit,
  Bathe my trembling heart and brow;
Fill me with thy hallow'd presence,
  Come, oh, come and fill me now.

Cho.—Fill me now, fill me now,
  Jesus, come, and fill me now;
Fill me with thy hallow'd presence,—
  Come, oh, come and fill me now.

2 Thou canst fill me, gracious Spirit,
  Though I cannot tell thee how;
But I need thee, greatly need thee,
  Come, oh, come and fill me now.

3 I am weakness, full of weakness;
  At thy sacred feet I bow;
Blest, divine, eternal Spirit,
  Fill with power, and fill me now.

4 Cleanse and comfort; bless and save me;
  Bathe, oh, bathe my heart and brow!
Thou art comforting and saving,
  Thou art sweetly filling now.
  —Rev. E. H. Stokes, D.D.

236. It is Good to be Here. (Copyr't.)

While we bow in thy name,
  Oh, meet us again,
Fill our hearts with the light of thy love;
  May the Spirit of grace,
  And the smiles of thy face,
Gently fall on us now from above.

Ref.—:|: It is good to be here, :|:
Thy perfect love now drives away all our fear,
And light streaming down makes the path way all clear.
  It is good for us, Lord, to be here.

2 Our souls long for thee;
  Oh, may we now see
A sin-cleansing blood-wave appear;
  And feel, as it rolls
  In power o'er our souls.
It is good for us, Lord, to be here.

3 Thou art with us, we know;
  We feel the sweet flow
Of the sin-cleansing wave's gladd'ning tide;
  We are washed from our sin,
  Made all holy within,
And in Jesus we sweetly abide.
  —Rev. I. N. Wilson.

237. Sunshine in the Soul. (Copyr't.)

There's sunshine in my soul to-day,
  More glorious and bright
Than glows in any earthly sky,
  For Jesus is my light.

Cho.—Oh, there's sunshine, blessed sunshine,
  When the peaceful, happy moments roll;
When Jesus shows his smiling face
  There is sunshine in the soul.

2 There's music in my soul to-day,
  A carol to my King,
And Jesus, listening, can hear
  The songs I cannot sing.

3 There's springtime in my soul to-day,
  For when the Lord is near
The dove of peace sings in my heart,
  The flowers of grace appear.

4 There's gladness in my soul to-day,
  And hope, and praise, and love,
For blessings which he gives me now,
  And joys "laid up" above.
  —E. E. Hewitt.

238. Jesus is Passing By. (Copyr't.)

Come, contrite one, and seek his grace,
  Jesus is passing by;
See in his reconciled face
  The sunshine of the sky.

Cho.—Passing by, passing by,
  Hasten to meet him on the way,
Jesus is passing to-day,
  Passing by, passing by.

2 Come, hungry one, and tell your need,
  Jesus is passing by;
The Bread of Life your soul will feed,
  And fully satisfy.

3 Come, weary one, and find sweet rest,
  Jesus is passing by;
Come where the longing heart is bless'd,
  And on his bosom lie.

4 Come, burdened one, bring all your care,
  Jesus is passing by;
The love that listens to your prayer,
  Will "no good thing" deny.
  —E. E. Hewitt.

239. I Know it is There.

F. M. D.   "Written in the Lamb's book of life."—Rev. xxi: 27.   Frank M. Davis.

1. I re-joice now to know that my sins are for-giv'n, That my name's on the book kept by an-gels in heav'n.
2. Je-sus sav'd me from sin and from all earthly strife, And has written my name in the Lamb's book of life.
3. Glo-ry be to the Lamb that for sinners was slain! He has written my name as one cleans'd from all stain.

CHORUS.
Yes, I know it is there on those pa-ges so fair, Written there, ... written there.

Copyright by Frank M. Davis. John J. Hood, owner.

Music No. 35 in "Unfading Treasures."

240   **More about Jesus.** (*Copyright.*)

MORE about Jesus would I know,
More of his grace to others show;
More of his saving fulness see,
More of his love who died for me.

Cho.—|: More, more about Jesus; :|
More of his saving fulness see,
More of his love who died for me.

2 More about Jesus let me learn,
More of his holy will discern;
Spirit of God, my teacher be,
Showing the things of Christ to me.

3 More about Jesus; in his word,
Holding communion with my Lord;
Hearing his voice in every line,
Making each faithful saying mine.

4 More about Jesus; on his throne,
Riches in glory all his own;
More of his kingdom's sure increase;
More of his coming, Prince of Peace.
—E. E. Hewitt.

Music No. 25 in "Unfading Treasures."

241   **Jesus is Good to Me.** (*Copyr't.*)

I LOVE my Saviour, his heart is good,
He has loved me o'er and o'er;
He sought me wand'ring, I'm saved by his blood,
And I love him more and more.

Cho.—|: Jesus is good to me; :|
So good! so good!
Jesus is good to my soul.

2 He calls, I rise, and he maketh me whole,
How fond his tender embrace!
He cleanses and keeps me and blesses my soul,
My day the smile of his face.

3 I want to love him with all my heart,
Though all its powers are small;
I will not keep from him any part,
For he is worthy of all.

4 He's good to me in my sorrow's night,
He's good in the tempest's roll;
He bringeth from darkness into light,—
With joy he filleth my soul.
—E. H. Stokes, D.D.

Music No. 149 in "Unfading Treasures."

242   The Haven of Rest. *(Copyr't.)*

My soul in sad exile was out on life's sea,
So burdened with sin, and distrest,
Till I heard a sweet voice saying, make me your choice;
And I entered the "Haven of Rest!"

Cho.—I've anchored my soul in the haven of rest,
I'll sail the wide seas no more;
The tempest may sweep o'er the wild, stormy deep,
In Jesus I'm safe evermore.

2 I yielded myself to his tender embrace,
And faith taking hold of the word,
My fetters fell off and I anchored my soul;
The haven of rest is my Lord.

3 The song of my soul, since the Lord made me whole,
Has been the OLD STORY so blest
Of Jesus, who'll save whosoever will have
A home in the "Haven of Rest!"

4 How precious the thought that we all may recline,
Like John the beloved and blest,
On Jesus' strong arm, where no tempest can harm,—
Secure in the "Haven of Rest!"

5 Oh, come to the Saviour, he patiently waits
To save by his power divine;
Come, anchor your soul in the haven of rest,
And say, "my Beloved is mine."
—H. L. Gilmour.

Music No. 271 in "Unfading Treasures."

243   Keep Close to Jesus. *(Copyr't.)*

When you start for the land of heavenly rest,
Keep close to Jesus all the way;
For he is the Guide, and he knows the way best,
Keep close to Jesus all the way.

Cho —:|: Keep close to Jesus. :|
Keep close to Jesus all the way; right,
By day or by night never turn from the
Keep close to Jesus all the way.

2 Never mind the storms or trials as you go,
Keep close to Jesus all the way;
'Tis a comfort and joy his favor to know.
Keep close to Jesus all the way.

3 To be safe from the darts of the evil one,
Keep close to Jesus all the way;
Take the shield of faith till the victory is won,
Keep close to Jesus all the way.

4 We shall reach our home in heaven by and bye,
Keep close to Jesus all the way;
Where to those we love we'll never say good-bye,
Keep close to Jesus all the way.
—John Lane.

Music No. 122 in "Unfading Treasures."

244   At the Cross. *(Copyright.)*

Alas! and did my Saviour bleed,
And did my Sovereign die?
Would he devote that sacred head
For such a worm as I?

Cho.—At the cross, at the cross,
Where I first saw the light,
And the burden of my heart rolled away,
It was there by faith
I received my sight,
And now I am happy all the day.

2 Was it for crimes that I had done,
He groaned upon the tree?
Amazing pity, grace unknown,
And love beyond degree!

3 But drops of grief can ne'er repay
The debt of love I owe;
Here, Lord, I give myself away,
'Tis all that I can do!
—I. Watts.

Music No. 90 in "Love and Praise No. 1."

245   He is Mine, I am His. *(Copyr't.)*

Blessed Lily of the Valley, oh, how fair is he!
He is mine, I am his;
Sweeter than the angel's music is his voice to me,
He is mine, I am his.
Where the lilies fair are blooming by the waters calm,
There he leads me, and upholds me by his strong right arm;
All the air is love around me, I can feel no harm,
He is mine, I am his.

Cho.—Lily of the valley, he is mine!
Lily of the valley, I am his!
Sweeter than the angel's music is his voice to me,
He is mine, I am his.

2 Let me sing of all his mercies, of his kindness true,
He is mine, I am his;
Fresh at morn, and in the evening, comes a blessing new,
He is mine, I am his!
With the deep'ning shadows comes a whisper, "safely rest!
Sleep in peace, for I am near thee, naught shall thee molest;
I will linger till the morning, keeper, friend and guest,"
He is mine, I am his.

3 Tho' he lead me thro' the valley of the shade of death,
He is mine, I am his;
Should I fear, when, oh, so tenderly he whispereth,
He is mine, I am his!
For the sunshine of his presence doth illume the night,
And he leads me thro' the valley to the mountain height;
Out of bondage into freedom, into cloudless light,
He is mine, I am his.
—Grace Elizabeth Cobb.

246. As Now We Part.

IDA SCOTT TAYLOR. J. HOWARD ENTWISLE.

1. God bless the hearts be-fore him here, And bless this hour so sweet;
   God bless and hold us each most dear Un-til a-gain we meet.
2. While seasons swift-ly come and go, And tears and smiles abound,
   God help us all in grace to grow, With love encompass'd round.
3. God bless to us his precious Word, And make its meaning clear,
   And let each heart a-new be stirr'd To worship in his fear.
4. Now voice with voice, and soul with soul We pray to meet a-gain,
   While loud and long the ech-oes roll, And sound the great a-men.

CHORUS. *Not too fast.*

As now we part God bless each heart, His grace your ev'ry need sup-ply;

rit. ad lib.

In all we do, God keep us strong and true, Dear friends, good-bye, good-bye.

Copyright, 1898, by John J. Hood.

INDEX.

Titles in CAPITALS; First lines in Roman type.

	HYMN.		HYMN.		HYMN.
A BETTER DAY COM-.	72	Come, Holy Spirit, h.	229	HAVE YE RECEIVED	154
A charge to keep I	217	Come, sinner, come	91	Heart and voice uni-	192
A FEAST OF LOVE TO-	151	Come, sinner, to the.	129	Hear the Master call-	122
Again in all his beau-	27	Come to the Saviour	152	HEAR THE MASTER'S	166
A glorious song is r..	44	Come, ye sinners,	230	HE FILLS IT ALL,	47
A hand all bruis'd and	185	Come, ye that love the	218	He hath set his love.	82
A HANDFUL OF CHEER	9	COMING TO JESUS,	204	HE IS CALLING,	228
Alas! and did my Sav-	244	CROSSING ONE BY ONE	20	HE IS MINE, I AM HIS	245
A LIGHT AT THE RIV-	188	CROWN HIM LORD OF	211	HE LOVETH MY SOUL,	116
A LIGHT IN OUR FA-	55			HE PAYS ME RIGHT A-	95
A little while to wait	79	DEEPER YET,	225	HE'S ALWAYS THE S.	31
All along the wayside	115	Do not draw the cur-	153	HE SAVES COMPLETE-	145
All hail the power	211	Don't go half-way w.	6	HIGHER GROUND,	89
ALL MY TRUST IN JE-	56	DON'T LOOK AT THE W	136	Hold on to God,	83
All the fields are gr.	166	DON'T YOU KNOW HE	149	Holy Spirit from a-	68
All the way the Sav-	8	Dost thou know at thy	187	HOSANNA! BLESS HIS	127
A MESSAGE FOR MOTH-	182	Dost thou love me, I.	62	Hover o'er me,	235
A message sweet is b.	42	Do your best while l.	12	How oft as we jour-.	9
And can I yet delay.	216	Draw me still closer,	25		
Are you going away.	43	DWELLING IN LOVE,	29	I am dwelling with .	139
Are you sowing, daily	97	Dying with Jesus, .	4	I am safe in the Rock	81
ARE YOU SOWING FOR	97			I AM SHELTERED IN T	81
As NOW WE PART,	246	Encamped along the	172	I asked thee, Lord, for	70
AT THE CROSS,	244			I came to Jesus with	127
		FAITH IS THE VICTO-	172	I do not know why tr	78
Behold! a royal army	16	Father, thou art will-	130	If o'er thy way dark	77
Behold the ark of G.	177	FILL TO OVERFLOW-	110	I have a friend to wh	202
Be not afraid,	18	FILL ME NOW,	235	I have found a friend	92
Be of good cheer,	51	FLASH THE TOPL'GTS	49	I have found a prec-.	157
Bethany's Comforter	117	From Calv'ry's moun	201	I HAVE FOUND JESUS,	101
Beyond the stars that	183	FULL AND FREE,	111	I have found the bless-	101
Blessed Bible.	75	FULLY JUSTIFIED,	13	I have found the wa-	30
Blessed Lily of the V.	245			I KNOW IT IS THERE,	239
Blessed words that w	137	Give me the mind of.	67	I'LL GO WHERE YOU .	148
BOUGHT ON CALVARY	144	GLADLY I WILL ANSW	62	I'll l've for him,	227
Bring your sins to the	120	GLORIOUS VICTORY,	161	I'LL STAND UP FOR H	132
BY GRACE ALONE,	42	GOD BLESS MY BOY,	102	I LOVE HIM FAR BET-	198
		God bless the hearts	246	I love my Saviour, his	241
Can it be that Jesus.	39	GOING AWAY WITH-.	43	I'M GOING TO MEET H	27
CARING FOR ME,	71	GOD'S THREE HUN-	80	I'm not afraid of the	133
Christ has shed his b	1-3	GREAT DELIVERER,	157	I'm pressing on the .	89
Christ lived and suf-	155			I'M WASHED IN THE B	33
COME, BROTHER, AND	88	HAPPY ALL THE DAY,	124	I never weary trav-	125
Come, contrite one,	238	Hark! hark, the trum-	50	IN GOD'S OWN TIME.	77
Come, Holy Spirit, c.	214	HASTE THEN TO JE-.	140	In love divine I dwell	29

SONGS OF LOVE AND PRAISE No. 5.

IN THAT CITY, . . 173	LOOK AND BE SAVED, 26	Once a sinner far fr.. 100
In the blood from the 225	Look unto him who h 46	Once, Gideon at God's 80
In the fight against s. 41	Look unto me and be 26	Once I stood by the . 190
In the shadow of his 145	Lord, for to-morrow a 159	Once I was heavy la- 124
In the rosy morning h 98	Lord, I care not for . 231	ONCE MORE, . . 160
In the shelter of the S. 194	LORD, I'M COMING H. 53	Once Peter took a ste 136
INTO HIS MARVEL- . 59	Lord Jesus, thou kn. 74	Once upon a stormy o 205
I read that whosoever 7	LOST AFTER ALL, . 113	One sweet hour, . 32
I rejoice now to know 239		ONLY BELIEVE,. . 18
I sat within a home . 206	Many weary miles . 182	ONLY ONCE YOU PASS 12
I SHALL BE LIKE HIM, 23	March on, happy sol- 24	On mem'ries' wall en- 107
IS MY NAME WRITTEN 231	MOMENT BY MOMENT 4	ON THAT SHORE, . 112
IS-TO-BE, . . 183	More about Jesus, . 240	On the band of trust- 63
IT IS GOOD TO BE H.. 236	My blest Redeemer i. 109	On the floods of de- . 60
It may not be on the 148	My country! 'tis of t. 209	ON THE HALLELUJAH 76
It pays to serve Jesus 198	MY GUIDE, . . 133	On the mighty Rock 94
I've a blessing every 121	My Jesus, I love thee 232	ON THE VICTORY SIDE 223
I've been a wand'rer 200	My life is full of sun- 95	ON THE WAY, . . 195
I've wandered far a-. 53	My life, my love I give 227	ON TO VICTORY, . 50
I WAS DOWN AT THE 190	My many sins are all 33	OPEN ALL THE DAY,. 179
I WILL SAY YES TO J. 200	MY MOTHER'S FACE,. 107	OPEN THE DOOR FOR 118
	My Saviour bore the 105	O the brightness and 165
JESUS, FOREVER THE 46	MY SAVIOUR FIRST OF 171	O the glory hallelujah 76
Jesus has saved me,. 128	MY SAVIOUR IS A FR. 92	Our friends on earth 234
JESUS IS ALL THAT Y. 152	My sins I've laid at . 88	Our hopes, like the r. 31
JESUS IS GOOD TO ME, 241	My soul, be on thy g. 219	Our souls cry out, . 223
Jesus is my joy and . 123	My soul in sad exile 242	OUR STRENGTH AND 24
Jesus, keep us till we 180	My soul, stay not in . 21	OUT BEYOND THE BR. 143
JESUS LEADS. . . 199		Out of Christ, . . 135
JESUS THE LIGHT OF 128	NEARER, EVERY DAY 28	Out to sea midst stor 49
Jesus, the loving Shep 170	Nearer, my God, to . 208	O WHY STAND YE I- . 40
Jesus, the name, . 210	NEVER SAY NO TO JE- 41	O WONDROUS CROSS, . 105
JESUS PROMISED ME A 146	No danger can my s. 73	
JOURNEY IN THE K.. 58	NO, NOT ONE, . . 11	PENTECOST, . . 63
JOY AND SUNSHINE, . 123	Not a cloud to hide . 181	Prayer is the key, . 197
Joy is beaming in my 132	NOTHING BUT MERCY 109	PRECIOUS LOVE, . 74
Just as I am, . . 213		
JUST FOR TO-DAY, . 159	O beautiful home of . 90	REDEEMED THRO TH. 194
JUST LEAVE IT ALL W 144	O bless the Lord, wh 195	RESTING BY THE WAY 162
Just one touch,. . 37	O brother, have you . 203	ROLL BACK THE SHAD- 153
	O brother, if the Lord 169	
KEEP CLOSE TO JE- . 243	O COME JUST NOW, . 129	SAFE FOREVERMORE, 94
KEEP US TILL WE M. 180	O'er death's sea, in y 173	Sailing down the str. 181
	O'er the dark and st. 112	SAILING IN THE ARK, 60
Lead me, Saviour, . 167	O'er the trackless d.. 150	Saviour, guide me d. 142
Lead on, . . . 138	OH, DON'T YOU HEAR 185	Saviour, hear me, wh 96
LEAN ON JESUS AND 87	OH, IT IS WONDERFUL 39	Saviour, lead me, lest 167
LET CHRIST COME IN 19	Oh, spread the tidings 184	Seeking the lost, . 108
LET THE SAVIOUR IN 178	Oh, the best friend to 196	SEND THE FIRE JUST 168
Let us be triumphant 5	Oh, the best songs of 147	SINCE CHRIST THE L. 73
LIFE AT THE CROSS,. 91	Oh, what a sad time 140	SINNERS ARE COMING 203
Like as a bird at even- 87	Oh, where is my fa- . 66	SITTING AT THE W. . 30
Like a shepherd, ten- 199	OH, WON'T YOU MEET 189	Some day, I know not 226
Like the sunshine br. 45	O idler, why loiter . 40	Some day we shall be 93
List to the story, . 174	OLD JORDAN'S WAVES 226	SONGS ABOUT JESUS, 147
Living for Jesus only, 119	O mourner in Zion, . 224	SOON I SHALL KNOW, 78
LIVING WATER, . 137	On Calvary's mount- 116	Sow kind deeds, . 54

222

Standing on the prom- 233	There'll be joy, . 45	When from every l. . 106
Stand up, stand up for 221	There's a blessed Str. 178	When I hear the tr. . 126
STEP OUT ON THE P.. 224	There's a day of glad- 10	When I shall reach . 23
SUNLIGHT ALL THE W 165	There's a deep, turbid 188	When I survey the w 215
SUNSHINE HAS COME 163	There's a hand that's 134	When I walk thro' t. 61
SUNSHINE IN THE S.. 237	There's a place in hea 146	When Jesus died on . 111
SUNSHINE OF THE S. 22	There's a song of hope 72	WHEN LIFE IS END-. 104
SWEETER AS THE DA. 48	There's a wideness in 228	When my life work . 171
Sweetly I'm resting in 176	There's gain for all o. 65	When shining stars t. 102
	There's not a friend l. 11	When storms are sw. 114
TELL HIM ALL, . . 120	There's sunshine in . 237	When the cares of life 104
TELL THEM THAT YO 175	The road we must tr. 38	WHEN THE ROLL IS . 52
THAT MEANS ME, . 7	THE SAVIOUR LEADS 8	When the skies are l. 69
THE ARK FLOATETH. 177	The Saviour lives w. 47	When the trumpet of 52
THE BEST FRIEND IS J 196	THE SAVIOUR WALKS 125	When we leave earth's 84
THE BLESSING AND T 70	The snow was drift-. 103	WHEN WE REACH O.. 181
THE BLOOD IS ON THE 17	THE SONG THAT NEV- 44	When your spirit b. . 149
The blood of Jesus s. 17	THE STREETS OF GOLD 69	When you stand amo 175
The clouds no longer 163	THE SUNNY SIDE OF . 5	When you start for t. 243
THE COMFORTER HAS 184	THE SWEET GLAD T.. 35	WHERE HE LEADETH 191
THE CROSS IS NOT GR. 186	THE VOICE ABOVE T. 85	Where my Shepherd 191
The cross that he ga. 186	THE WONDERFUL S. 1-3	Wheresoe'er we be o. 55
The dear old story of 48	This life will soon be 189	WHERE WILT THOU . 131
THE GOLDEN KEY, . 197	Thro' our faith in C. 13	While life prolongs,. 212
THE GOOD SHEPHERD 103	Through the valley, . 61	While upon the pil-. 162
The God of Jacob will 83	'Tis sad to think, that 113	While we bow in thy 236
THE HALLELUJAH SID 100	Toiler in the harvest 64	While we now, dear 168
THE HAVEN OF REST, 242	To my blessed Lord . 28	WHO CAN TELL? . 66
THE HARBOR LIGHTS 150	TRY TO SAVE SOME O. 99	WHOSOEVER BELIEV- 201
THE HARBOR HOME,. 156		Who will answer for 34
THE HEIGHTS OF BEU- 139	VICTORY IS NIGH, . 115	WHO WILL GO TO-D.. 122
THE HOME-COMING, . 84	Victory, victory, glo- 161	WHY DON'T YOU TELL 169
THE JOYFUL SONG, . 16	Vile and sinful tho' . 56	Will you be one, . 14
THE KNOCK OF THE N 187		WILL YOU GO?. . 141
THE LIFE ON WINGS, 21	WAITING AT THE M. 130	With hearts attuned 160
THE LIGHTS OF THE . 38	WAITING ON BEFORE 64	With joyful hope I . 71
THE LORD KNOWETH 155	WAIT ON THE LORD, 15	With penitence I co.. 204
THE MANTLE OF LOVE 164	We are on the win-. . 57	Wonderful mercy th. 59
The morning light is 220	WE'LL MEET THEM,. 90	WORDS OF HEARTF'T 202
THE OLD FOLK'S HYM 206	WE'LL NEVER SAY . 234	WORK FOR JESUS, . 98
The pearly gates of g. 179	We're trav'ling home 141	Work for the night is 222
THE PENITENT'S PLE 96	WE SHALL BE SATIS- 93	Would Jesus live in . 158
The promise assures . 86	We shall cross the m. 20	Would you go rejoic- 58
THE PROMISE IS DA-. 86	We shall reach the l. 35	Would you to your S. 19
There is a beautiful h 144	WE WILL MARCH A-. 106	Wounded and dying 99
There is a danger line 143	What a friend we h. 207	
There is a voice above 85	WHAT SHALL OUR R. 134	Ye are the temples . 154
There is sunshine for 22	WHAT WOULD JESUS 158	YOU ARE INVITED TO 10
There'll be no dark v. 36	When darkness is h. 118	You're sailing t'ward 156

www.ingramcontent.com/pod-product-compliance
Lightning Source LLC
Chambersburg PA
CBHW031819220426
43662CB00007B/708